John Matthias was born in 1941 in Columbus, Ohio. For many years he taught at the University of Notre Dame, but also spent long periods of time in the UK, both at Cambridge and at his wife's childhood home in Hacheston, Suffolk. He has been a Visiting Fellow in poetry at Clare Hall, Cambridge, and is now a Life Member. Until 2012 he was poetry editor of *Notre Dame Review* and is now Editor at Large. Matthias has published some thirty books of poetry, translation, scholarship, and collaboration. His most recent books are *New Selected Poems*, (2004), *Kedging* (2007), *Trigons* (2010), *Collected Shorter Poems Vol 2, Collected Longer Poems* (all verse) and *Who Was Cousin Alice? And Other Questions* (2011) (mostly prose). In 1998 Robert Archambeau edited *Word Play Place: Essays on the poetry of John Matthias*, and in 2011 Joe Francis Doerr published a second volume of essays on his work, *The Salt Companion to the Poetry of John Matthias*. His complete poems have now been published in three volumes by Shearsman: *Collected Longer Poems* (2012), and *Collected Shorter Poems* in two volumes (2011 and 2013).

Also by John Matthias

Poetry
Bucyrus (1970)
Turns (1975)
Crossing (1979)
Bathory & Lermontov (1980)
Northern Summer (1984)
A Gathering of Ways (1991)
Swimming at Midnight (1995)
Beltane at Aphelion (1995)
Pages: New Poems & Cuttings (2000)
Working Progress, Working Title (2002)
Swell & Variations on the Song of Songs (2003)
New Selected Poems (2004)
Kedging (2007)
Trigons (2010)
Collected Shorter Poems, Vol. 2 (2011)
Collected Longer Poems (2012)

Translations
Contemporary Swedish Poetry (1980)
　(with Göran Printz-Påhlson)
Jan Östergren: Rainmaker (1983)
　(with Göran Printz-Påhlson)
The Battle of Kosovo (1987)
　(with Vladeta Vučković)
Three-Toed Gull: Selected Poems of Jesper Svenbro (2003)
　(with Lars-Håkan Svensson)

Essays
Reading Old Friends (1992)
Who Was Cousin Alice? and Other Questions (2011)

Editions
23 Modern British Poets (1971)
Introducing David Jones (1980)
David Jones: Man and Poet (1989)
Selected Works of David Jones (1992)
Notre Dame Review: The First Ten Years (2009)
　(with William O'Rourke)

Collected Shorter Poems

Vol. 1

1963–1994

John Matthias

Shearsman Books

Published in the United Kingdom in 2013 by
Shearsman Books Ltd
50 Westons Hill Drive
Emersons Green
BRISTOL
BS16 7DF

Shearsman Books Ltd Registered Office
30–31 St. James Place, Mangotsfield, Bristol BS16 9JB
(this address not for correspondence)

www.shearsman.com

ISBN 978-1-84861-279-2

Copyright © John Matthias, 1971, 1975, 1979, 1984, 2000, 2004, 2013.
Music copyright © David Isele, 2000.

The right of John Matthias to be identified as the author of this work
has been asserted by him in accordance with the
Copyrights, Designs and Patents Act of 1988.
All rights reserved.

Acknowledgements

The poems in this volume were first published as follows:
Bucyrus (Athens, OH: Swallow Press 1971);
Turns (London: Anvil Press Poetry 1975);
Crossing (London: Anvil Press Poetry 1979);
Northern Summer (London: Anvil Press Poetry 1984);
Pages: New Poems and Cuttings (Athens, OH: Swallow Press 2000);
New Selected Poems (Cambridge: Salt Publishing 2004).

The music reproduced here was first published as part of David Isele's
Four Songs for Voice by the E.C. Schirmer Music Company. Thanks to both
composer and publisher for permission to reprint the scores here.

Contents

For Diana: A Ballad, A Book   9

Part I: Early Poems (1) & Some from *Turns* (1975)
- Triptych   13
- From the Frau Trix Dürst-Hass Collection   15
- Female Nude, Young   16
- What They Say   17
- Painter Kinsey's Favorite Pages   18
- Song   19
- Swimming at Midnight   20
- Aubade   21
- Fragments for an Epithalamion   22
- Song   23
- Song: For an Isele Setting   24
- David Isele: 'Between'   25
- Song: Of a Lady Long Gone   29
- Song: Intonations   30
- Song: Into the Bargain   31
- Fathers   32
- Uncle   34
- Survivors   35
- Edward   37
- Part of an Answer   39
- Reply to a Valentine   40
- If Not a Technical Song American   41
- Kent State University: May 4, 1970   43
- Nightmare After Mandelstam   45
- U.S.IS. Lecturer   46
- For John, After His Visit: Suffolk, Fall   48

Part II: Poems 1975-1980 (1)
- A Dedication   55
- Homing Poem   56
- Dissemblers with Their Prince   57
- Spokesman to Bailiff, 1349: Plague   58
- Having heard how great was the fame…   59
- Variations on a Theme by Horace   61
- After Ekelöf   64

Void Which Falls Out of Void	65
August	66
Dunwich: Winter Visit Alone	68
Once for English Music	69
59 Lines Assembled Quickly…	72
26 June 1381/1977	75
Brandon, Breckland: The Flint Knappers	79
Words for Sir Thomas Browne	82
Lines for the Gentlemen	86
More Lines for the Gentlemen	88
My Youngest Daughter…	90
Mark Twain in the Fens	91
Paul Verlaine in Lincolnshire	93
You Measure John	95
On the Death of Benjamin Britten	96
An East Anglian Poem	97
Epilogue from a New Home	102

Part III: Poems 1975-1980 (2)

Double Invocation…	109
The Fen Birds' Cry	112
Evening Song	114
Two Ladies	115
Verrucas	118
Mostly Joan Poulson's Recipes, Etc.	120
After the Death of Chekhov	122
Friendship	123
Agape	125
Poem for Cynouai	126
Turns: Toward a Provisional Poetics and a Discipline	135
Double Derivation, Association, and Cliché	141
Clarifications for Robert Jacoby	147

Part IV: Poems 1975-1985

On a Slip of the Tongue	153
Words for Karl Wallenda	154
Three Around a Revolution	157
Born 1851, Henry Demuth	159
Bakunin in Italy	160
Zurich to London, Tzara to Trotsky	161

A Painter	162
Alexander Kerensky at Stanford	163
Five for Michael Anania	164
Double Sonnet on the Absence of Text	167
At a Screening of Gance's *Napoleon*	168
Unpleasant Letter	170
Two Poems in Dedication	173
Elegy for Clara	175
On Lake Michigan	177
Back in Columbus, Ohio	178
To Vladeta Vučković	179
Three Derivations	187
In Praise of Fire	189
Two Derivations	190
Fifteen Derivations	192
From a Visit to Dalmatia, 1978	196
Two Poems	198
Fragments after Hamsun	199
Free Translation and Recombination	200
A Wind in Roussillon	203

Part V: Four Monologues and a Song Cycle

The Old Master's Plaine Style Complainte	213
A Cambridge Spinning House	218
Mr. Rothenstein's Rudiments	223
Auto Icon	227
Song Cycle Awaiting a Setting	230

Part VI: Early Poems (2)

I Gather the Bones of *Bucyrus*	237
Two Graffiti	238
Smoking Cigars with a Friend	239
Diptych	241
Five Alchemical Lyrics	242
Herman's Poems	245
Arzeno Kirkpatrick	250
The Crazy Side of the Room	251
Song for a David Isele Setting	252
David Isele: 'A Dazzle Once'	253
Three Love Songs for U.P.I.	258

Statement	260
Missed Call	262
Graffiti Gratis Bon Obscène Maudit d'Autrefois	263
Short Parts of a Long Poem	265
Notes	278

For Diana: A Ballad, A Book

I had in my charge two ladies
And I was the King of the West.
I had in my charge two ladies
And two of Angloria's best.

And the wind beat the rain at the window.
And the wind beat the rain on the stair.
I bolted the doors and compartments.
I took down the ladies' bright hair.

And they set up a table, my beauties,
They filled it with wine and delights.
Fulfilled and complete were my duties;
Reward was an eon of nights.

And the wind beat the rain at the window
And the wind beat the rain on the stair.
We ate and we drank and we drank and we ate
And we finished our banqueting there.

And I belched and arose from the table,
I swallowed a pickled red pear,
I hurried as fast as I'm able
To strip me a lady bare . . .

When suddenly face at the window,
Suddenly foot at the stair,
Suddenly sound of an army around
And a voice that split open the air.

It said: I'm the King of the West.
It said: You failed your quest.
Hand over your beauties
Go back to your duties
Get out and work with the rest.

Oh I was sent out in the wind and the rain
And I never set foot in that country again.

Part I

Early Poems (1)

&

Some from *Turns* (1975)

Triptych

1

He doesn't sleep. He sits.
He looks around.
Afraid of quiet, bits
Of dust and sound,
He doesn't sleep. He sits
And looks around.
He was in love, he thinks.
He cannot smile.
He reads his early peoms
To learn his style.
He doesn't write. He was
In love. He thinks.
He scribbles at a pad
With colored inks.

2

There is no bed. One stands.
One walks about.
A fountain for the hands
Drips water out.
There is no pillow, sheet,
Or bed at all;
A fountain for the feet
Is in the hall.
A fountain for the feet
Or for the hands—
Oh, sit upon the floor!
A yellow needle
Pins a ballad to
The door.

3

The King was dead. Earth flat.
And women real.
Beside me Marcus sat.
We took our meal.
"I have his daughter, sir,
I have his bride.
A proper poem, my Lord,
Will buy them tied.
A proper poem, my Lord,
If you can write.
I'll have them in your bed
Tomorrow night."
And I remember that.
And I recall.
Beside me Marcus sat
And that was all.

From the Frau Trix Dürst-Hass Collection
(& *Pädagogisches Skizzenbuch*)

                "Less is more"
                  Ludwig Mies von der Rohe

At night, alone, and sick
of anything the day
or sunlight had to kick
at him, that purple way
of his with purple fish
conceived a hook that may
have been a cloudy wish
or just a carless thought.

But either way, once caught,
those stricken eels took
the curious lance he'd tossed
them by its baited hook
and pulled him, silent, lost,
where only they had been before
so Bauhaus eyes could look
beyond the Skizzenbuch

& not at *yes* but *nevermore*.

                    (Paul Klee: 'The Seafarer,' 1923)

Female Nude, Young

Conscious of being
afraid or aware;
afraid of fearing
awareness or fear,
one can paint
colorful portraits of others.

Take that unrepentant
child there by the mirror. Take
those fallen scarlet flowers: Destroy,
hopeless with color, the flowers
the mirror the child.

Responsibility ends
and begins. Otherwise,
where have we been? And
what have we seen?

What They Say

They say that
Egon Schiele
drew from models
his onanistic nudes
and friends.

They lay on beds
touching themselves,
lithe. He painted
from a ladder
in his loft.

And it's perspective
that distorts
and the omissions:
the beds the girls
lay on, or the chairs.

The ladder and the beds
were Egon Schiele's.
The postures and
the gestures
were all theirs.

Painter Kinsey's Favorite Pages

Douglas Kinsey's favorite pages in the four
books of poetry I've given him
by Stevens, Lowell, Berryman, and Moore

are those that separate the sections.
There is nothing written on them at all
save for the Roman numerals,

I   II   III   IV

rather high and very black and
delicately right of center,
sliding oh so gently into winter.

Song

Handsome lovers know this place
and lovers knew it long ago.
Spirits whisper: love is grace.

I brought my beauty here in lace,
here to where the shadows grow,
and spirits whispered: love is grace.

Spirits whispered: love is grace
and all the lovers seemed to know.
I took my beauty in that place

as spirits whispered: love is grace.
My beauty did not find it so.
She gathered up her lace to go

and fled, angelic,
from my face…
Spirits whisper: love is grace.

Swimming at Midnight

[Near my grandparents' home at the outskirts of town, a stone quarry was established, then abandoned, nearly a hundred and fifty years ago. The early blasting hit water, and after many soundings were taken, the management concluded that they had uncovered a bottomless lake, fed, they surmised, by a sizable underground river.]

Under a pine and confusion:
oh! Tangles of clothes: (come
on, silly, nobody's here:) and
naked as fish, a boy and a girl.
(Nobody comes here: nobody looks:
nobody watches us watching us
watch.) Except the police.
Thighs slide into the moon.
Humbly, into the stars: Mirrored,
flashes a father's red eye, a
blue-bitten mother's red lip: No
Swimming Allowed In The Quarry
At Night. (Anyway, nevertheless
and moreover: feel how warm!) here,
among the reflections. (Feel the
water's mouth and its hands, feel
them imitate mine: can there truly
be any danger?) danger allowed in
the quarry at night? can people
really have drowned? (Now my body
is only water alive, and aeons
ago you were a fish growing
legs—) well, dust to dust, a
curious notion. But quarry water on
dust green with seed! Quarry water
forbidden on land after dark! What
young forms of vegetation emerge.
What new colors of light.

Aubade

Listen: the city's alive: they're
selling the apples and wine
of a day and a night.
Drummer is playing a drum
in the street, somebody dances
and somebody sings—someone's
hawking copper pots & pans.

Listen: (ah, you're sleeping still)
but listen, listen anyway, or dream:
All of this is gift, improbable and
chance: it's inadvertence, accident
and all that slips the mind.

Unlikely is the gentle
sleep you sleep; unlikely are
the simple sounds, the bending dawn,
my arms; unlikely and absurd
that we are here.

Dear girl,
against the certainties
what hour? What day?
How make what accident
and chance what rule?

Fragments for an Epithalamion

…in lieu of ornaments,
a wedding song. No angels can I summon
and no swans; no maidens, no, nor drunken
dancing boys. I summon this:

        remembered seas and silences

in the quiet of the dusk there will
be ceremony soon and there was
ceremony of uncertain kind before.
Silent by a silent sea did we see minstrels
in the surf who sang?

        This stillness summons
absent things like time…

        like angels, maidens,
dancing boys, and swans

Song

Sound of people playing tennis
in the little park.
A neighbor practicing her violin,
sunbeams through a window.

Anyday, anyday. This day too.

An agreeable letter
from a poet I respect.
A sentence in an old friend's book,
I love my life.

This day too. Or anyday.

The present *does* compel us.
How I'd like, old friend, to say
I love my life. I have.

The cat rolls over, stretches
out its hind legs in a beam of sun.
The violinist
and the tennis players play.

Song: For an Isele Setting

Between here
and away
is a
way

And a point
to be made

What matter
now
is how?

To leave is
to the point

It is

It is a way

(And equally
the coffee
and the
calm)

Between

Song: Of a Lady Long Gone

Mosquitoes buzz and flies
and it is hot, and is
afraid who waits, bathed

and scented, lilacs
braided in her hair. *Can
Walk away. Can disappear.*

*Can leave an empty garret
and a key.* Across the
lake the city glitters

light. (Who waits and
listens, listening is
afraid.) *To leave the*

*door ajar and nothing
there. To put a lantern
out & drink the rain.* She

naked is her body is her
cry. (Insects ticking at
a pane.) *Can walk away:*

I'll walk away. She is
her death, His phallus
on her thigh. Across the

lake the city glitters light.
I'll walk, she says, *the
quiet waters by.*

Song: Intonations

Strange that I
should say
it your way
"*Are* you asleep"
to her
and after all
this time
and after all

Are you asleep?
(a stupid question)
No she says
I'm not
and then she
turns and yawns
and then
she is

Are you asleep?
I wonder where…
I wonder why
your voice is
in my mouth

Song: Into the Bargain

Stranger, agent, sinister
shade, friend of my oldest
enemy's friends

Why do you follow me now
to railway stations
and airports?

Why is it always
you in the taxi,
gondola, rickshaw?

Open, kindly, to
somebody else's
terrified eyes

Your travel brochures

Fathers

I never knew them.
Neither one. That
ancient Englishman
was deaf and in-
accessible—I

took his daughter
from his house.
He was dreaming
of ships, of Vienna,
his German assassin

sleeping under
his bed:
I never knew.
In Republican
Ohio, the man

I thought I
hated grew so
thin he'd slip
he said a wedding
band around his

upper arm. Rheumatic,
he rode like a horse
his electrical in-
valid chair.
He was a judge

and should have
been a sailor…
Who'd stand no
nonsense, tell
them of the Empire

and by God Britannia,
chew his pipe
and try to
understand his girl—
twenty-one and

born when
he was fifty.
And if I'd known them,
ether one, if I'm a
sailor now and should

have been a judge,
what son will talk
to me? What stranger
take my daughter from
a father's house?

Uncle

You were our antique toy
from the twenties, a wealthy
visitor from Dayton who
arrived on Saturdays and

passed out dollar bills.
Your nephews liked you drunk.
"A way of life" you told us—
and sang, basso profundo,

all your fraternity songs.
Before you made your million
you sold balloons to kids
and waited for the war you

didn't fight to lift you,
pickled, out of the depression.
And now you have a day nurse
and a night nurse.

When my father died, the best
you managed was: "They had
to stick his pecker in
the pot for months."

And my father in a book he gave
his sister once (your wife):
"For Betty: who doesn't need
a gyroscope to keep her steady."

Survivors

1

A letter arrives in answer
to mine—but six years late…
"John," it says,
                "Dear John…" and

"I remember absolutely nothing.
What you say is probably
all true; for me those
years are blank. I believe
you when you say you knew
me then, that we were friends,
and yet I don't remember you
at all, or all those others
who had names, or anyone. You see,

the fittest don't survive—
it's the survivors."

2

Like old women, burying their
husbands, burying their sons, lasting
it out for years without their breasts
or wombs, with ancient eyes,
arthritic hands, and memories like
gorgeous ships they launch
despairingly to bring back all
their dead, and which, as if constructed
by some clumsy sonneteer, betray them
instantly and sink without a trace.

3

Or women not so old—
                but always
women, not the men who knock

their brains and bodies against
fatal obstacles and spit their blood
on pillows and their hearts on sleeves
at forty-five to die of being fit.

I've known a woman keep her watch
beside a bed of botched ambition
where her man lay down and took
five years to die…

And though I drove one January night
through freezing rain into Ohio—
and though I hurried,
seeking the words of the dying—
all I found was a turning circle of women,
all I heard was the lamentation of survivors.

Edward

And whatten penace wul ye drie?

Edward, Edward, how we fear the sick!
I think I can almost remember you
whose name I'm called, John Edward.
Your illness was a terror
for us all. We, your nephews, marveled
in our fear. We didn't know
exactly what the sick know, but we
knew they know—Oh things forbidden to the fit.
You were a kind of Shaman for us then.

We watched you jerk from chair
to cane, we watched you jam your gears, repeat,
walk backwards through the door,
then freeze and point, all man of ice,
at something moving after it had moved,
and then unfreeze, unlock,
and then repeat: *I do it then, I do it then.*

You gave us candies made of malted milk
and the family left you dying
in your corner chair. You had the post-war
sleeping-sickness, and you mostly slept:
through our lives, through your own.
There seemed no pity for you in that house.
For me, it was a magic time. I loved
my cousin then the way a boy of eight can
love a boy of ten. What could any of us do
for you? We took your candy and we fled.

Everybody fled: to their lunches or their jobs,
to their games or their affairs.
The other, boozy uncle said: *He was an ass-man once.*
For days I wondered what he meant.
Edward, did you curse us all the way you
might have, Shaman-like and darkly, silently:
So go off to your God-damned job and leave me here.

*Your lunch. Your girl. Kid, go ride your bike
into a fucking truck.* Who knows what you thought.
The children fled with the adults.

But when your brother in his final illness wept,
and when I had no pity, when I couldn't
stand to hear him say like any eight-year-old:
You made me cry, and when he said just audibly
 enough for me to hear*: Go back to your
God-damned books*, then, Edward, I thought
I could remember you almost
and me a book-man, not an ass-man, now.
Edward, Edward, *howe we fear our ain,
Sic counseils O
they give us of mortality.*

Part of an Answer

The man who forced the
window with a wrench
was never there. I
opened it myself: you
suffered anyway your

mugging and his lust.
If we really pulled
our knives in bed
and slashed, you'd
never ask. I'd never

say: responsibility
ends. Your piety!
I'll live on water
and dried peas.
Poems, love, poems!

I try to make the
evil things, secondary
worlds, though even
A Magus said it—primary
there—no world

but the world. And
The Word? A girl
who died for poetry
once wrote: *to crawl
between the lines*

of print and sleep. She
wanted that. Accretion
then, and possibility.
You wind your watch
and I attend.

Reply to a Valentine

I will hope you accept
my apologies. The delay.
The decay. Dangers may be
overstressed initially

or not. But I welcome
this interest of yours.
And I hymn: atlases and
herbals, occult power.

I have it all in a book
bound in iron. Can it be
computed can it quantify?
Quanta is it computation?

You ask. Me! Value error, see?
Incorrect command. Government
departments are involved with
overlapping annual leaves.

Should you forget yourself and
with yourself your station,
enter here litigious and ecstatic.
Your penetrating questions.

Citizens such as yourself.

Atlases and herbals.

Occult power.

If Not a Technical Song American: Statement, Harangue, and Narrative

1: STATEMENT

Just last night I read your poems to the President.
You don't believe me, but I really did.
He broke down completely and
wept all over his desk.
Now that I've done my work, you can relax.
Everything's going to be OK.

And I read your poems to a joint session of Congress.
I read your poems to the F.B.I. and the C.I.A.
Now that I've done my work, you can relax.
Everything's going to be OK.

2: HARANGUE

Your tired evasions, euphemism-lies.
Civilized man and his word-hoard.
Will you be relinquant
or relinquished?

Name and Title. Religion and Rank.
Put a check in the column.
Put a check in the bank.

If you'd be only a little bit clever.
If you'd be occasionally.
If you'd be forever.

If you'd be my government.
If you'd be my gal.
If you'd be my treason and my tongue.

If anything articulate remains,
Identify the numbers by the names.

3: Narrative

Cachetic, cachectic.
Heart rate grossly irregular.
Jugular venous distention.
Systolic expansile pulse.

Right ventricular lift.
Left ventricular tap.
Murmur along the sternal borders.
Pulmonary edema.

All piezometers installed
in the boreholes.
Static and dynamic
cone penetration made.

Infra red results
allow mathematical models.
I hope I was never
complacent: Seismology.

BUT IF I WAS IN LOVE WITH YOU?
I was in love with you, I think.
I think I didn't have the heart.
No, I never even thought to move the earth.

Kent State University: May 4, 1970

(i.m. Jeffrey Miller, Sandra Lee Scheuer,
Allison Krause, and Bill Schroeder)

1

May 4th and coming from
Chicago thinking '68 and
'68 afraid of getting shot and

now they have for saying things
got shot or their assembly or

because of other people's
notion of decorum

2

Passing the commuter stops,
Hyde Park, gray and weathered
houses by the block-house

high school walls: blackened
letters eight feet high among some

       lesser signals: SUICIDE

and all these voices saying, OK, OK

       they got what they deserved
       they got it like they ought

3

In the photograph you see the situation:
over someone's shoulder in the picture
in the paper: glance to the side and

       they'll blow out your brains

your cowboy fantasies: your justice that
would stare them down: and there they are, The Law,
and plug your people dead:

dead as door mice, dead as door mats
dead in spite of what they said or

what they only thought or guessed,
their silliness and smiles:

The other guys are faster, and they draw.

Nightmare After Mandelstam: Who Spoke of the Language Itself

(For Rory Holscher and John Hessler, May 1970)

I see America closing in on my friends.
Once I was angry; once I protested in poems.
Mandelstam: May 13, 1934: I see
the Kremlin's mountaineer in America.

Words, words: the poem an execution.
They are gunning for Rory and John.
I can see them come in the night.

There is no place to hide.
Their aim is single and passionate.
I see America closing in on my friends.

But I harbor them in my house
with my wife and my beautiful daughters.
There is a knock at the door,
the face of a goon at the window.

They will murder us, simply.
They have been elected to do it.
There is no motivation at all.
Our documents are simple and in order.

U.S.I.S. Lecturer
—*Amsterdam, Kalverstraat, March*

What I hear at first is *Heren* and then *Heroine*.
Then the sudden toothy Dutchman
ages dreadfully and vaguely threatens
something, turns American,
and says with perfect clarity: "Heroin,

like *smack*." We stare each other down.
Eyes gone, muscles gone, he is teeth & yellow paper.
Still, I sense he is about my age.
I brush on past him, mind all wheeling
backwards out of gear

to 1961 when I was here before and just eighteen.
What I dreamed into the streets of Amsterdam
was Love: pure, high, unyielding,
disdainful, and serene.
An appallingly beautiful bawd said she'd

take my friend and me together. He
went in alone, and for a moment I could see
them swimming in the gaudy lights
behind her fishbowl window. Someone opened up
a paper and I read: *Hemingway Zelfmoord*.

A decade and a half. I'm here to lecture twice
on a man who was my teacher once
who, that very afternoon, in hot America,
sat down aching and wrote out:
"My mother has your shotgun." And:

"It's so I broke down here."
In the middle of his poem, he meant.
I heard myself quote Woody Allen to a group
of students yesterday in Leiden when
they asked me what I thought they could believe in.

Sex and death, I said.
Part of me's gone rotten as my junkie-brother's eyes.
Respectful and respectable, I took
a check from my ambassador
and quoted Woody Allen's quip to get a laugh.

I forgot to say: "It was as he wrote his poem,
you understand. His father
had self-murdered too." Somewhere there,
in 1961 or so, was Love.
I'll think about the man who wrote the poem.

For John, After His Visit: Suffolk, Fall

Soldati's band shook Patty Fenelon's house
        last Spring so badly that the
Bookcase toppled down and spilled the cheap
        red wine on three authentic South
Bend, Indiana drunks....
                            For you, who love
        the elegiac and, if you believed
The arts you practice had in fact a chance
        of life at all, would prophesy
A new Romantic muse for all of us, how
        can I speak generously enough
About the life we've shared—the rich neurotic
        squalor of the Midwest's Catholic
Mecca (...you a convert, me a Roman guest—
        cloistered there together preaching
Culture to the grandsons of Italian immigrants,
        the sons of Irishmen and Poles)?

You must, you always told me,
        have intensity. Half your students
Always thought you mad. Like Gordon
        Liddy on a job you'd go
To them bewigged and bearded bearing with
        you some incongruous foreign
Object—a Henry James harpoon or a Melvillian
        top hat—while through the hidden
Speakers blared your tape of Colin Davis and
        the BBC crooning Elgar on the
Last night of the Proms. Light in darkness, John!
        And all your manic gestures were serene.

Yeats to Lady Gregory, Nineteen Hundred & Four:
        "I did not succeed at Notre Dame."
He began to think his notions seemed "the thunder
        of a battle in some other star"; the thought
Confused him and he lectured badly; later he
        told tales with the "merry priests."

So you were not the first to feel estranged! And
    oh the thunder of your battle in that
Other star, its foolishness and grace. Beyond that
    fiddle, though, intensity was real
Enough for both of us.

How was I to know, returning from the dusty
    attic room where I had gone, where
I had often gone from midnight until three, and
    seeing you stare vacantly across
Your desk and through your lighted study
    window at the February snow that
You should truly be in love with my young
    friend, with that same lonely girl?

Was that the week you thought your son was ill?
    When you waited frightened while the
Severed head of Johnny's Siamese cat melted grinning
    in its package of dry ice padlocked in
The Greyhound baggage room in Indianapolis?
    The tests were negative, the bites
And scratches healed....

                Hiking on a treadmill
    at the clinic, I tested badly on a
Winter afternoon myself. I traded polysyllables
    with cardiologists who hooked me to their
Apparatus, checked my pressures, watched my blips
    on television screens, and asked me all
The secrets of my heart....

Once we hiked together on the muddy banks of the
    St. Joseph, then across a farm. Your
Children ran ahead. They led you, while you
    talked in words they could not hear,
Haranguing me about the words you sometimes spoke
    when you would only speak, to credit
For a moment, because they looked at all around
    them, tree and bush and flower, because
They did not name and did not need to name, the
    eluctable modality of all you saw.

What more homely elegiacs, John, than this:
    reading backwards in a diary from
May—May to January, January twenty-fifth ... and
    all my pulses skip. My father's gestures
Of exhausted resignation cease; he drops his cup
    of Ovaltine and stares into my
Mother's eyes amazed.... No dream, even, did he
    send me in my mourning time, no news
At all... As a child I saw irregularities signaled
    in the pulsings of distended veins
Running up his temples and across his wrists:
    more *affaires de coeur*....
                            You made
Your trip among the dead ten years ago
    but found a Christian God along
The way in Barcelona. Did I take for politics
    Your strange Falangist quips
The day we met?

December last, a month before my father's death,
    a quiet Christmas eve with sentimental
And nostalgic talk, some caroling. Suddenly
    the blood. Stalking through a dark
And quiet house with automatic rifle and grenades
    you'd kick a bedroom door to bits and
Blast the sleeping couple in their bed, sprinkling
    holy water everywhere—your own obsessive
Dream. "I must have savagery," a wealthy British
    poet told me, leaving for the States.
I've gone the other way. My next door neighbor
    pounded at my door on Christmas eve; his
Bleeding wounds were real. What was all of England
    to a single one of his desires?
When I needed help you harbored me.

I wonder if our quarrel touches writing desks,
    like Mandelstam's with Pasternak. The
Harrowed man required none, the other poet did.
    Behind each artifact of any worth,
Cocteau insists, there is a house, a lamp, a fire,
    a plate of soup, a rack of pipes,

And wine. The bourgeoisie as bedrock. Mandelstam
    would crouch in corners listening to
The burning in his brain. If you're a Russian
    Jew because I am a wanton I am Catholic.

So what's the Devil's wage? Your riddling military
    metaphors unwind from Clausewitz and you
Will not say; your Faust, de Sade in neat quotations
    will not do. In London monographs on
Mahler are delivered in the morning post intended
    for the eyes of diplomats on holiday in
Devon—the still & deadly music of the IRA. One
    by one these books explode … In the hands
Of an unlucky clerk, the lap of an astonished secretary
    dreaming of her lover.

Stranger, then, and brother! John, these last three
    nights I've listened for you here,
Listened for you here where off the North Sea
    early Autumn winds bring down the
Twigs and bang the shutters of this house
    you came to bringing with you
Secrets and your difficult soul. "In disintegrating
    space we are an architecture of sounds."
And you are not returning.

Part II

Poems 1975–1980 (1)

i.m. Pamela Adams and Lois Kirkpatrick Matthias
and for a house:
Cherry Tree, Hacheston, Suffolk

A Dedication

Look at these words.
what is there in them
you should tolerate
my absences, my silence?

As if they made a world
where we could live, you
offer me what I expect.

Should least. Last. And
only look on circumspect.

Homing Poem

1

An acre, a rod,
And eleven
Perches of land

The stone walls
The thirteen towers

And all tithes
& corn & hemp & flax

The stone walls
The thirteen towers

2

An acre, a rod,
And eleven
Perches of land

The stone walls
The thirteen towers

And all tithes
& corn & hemp & flax

The stone walls
The thirteen towers

Dissemblers with Their Prince

Foxes and Firebrands!
Son of a heretic king,
His crafty council, his
Insidious design.

The Word itself in
Vulgar tongue disgusts.
Four square to the
Scaffold: Rood & Shrine!

Spokesman to Bailiff, 1349: Plague

("…after which the bourgeoisie.")

We leave you payment.
In a cup of vinegar
beside the well, the
coins that you require.

Let no one approach us.
Here we make an end
of ceremony, custom. In
our wreckage all of

Europe's racked, your
kindness unrequited in
its kind. And yet our death's
a birth of avarice and

powers oblique, unfathomed.
Leave us bread and ointments.
Free from obligations, we
leave the world to its wealth.

Having heard how great was the fame that
Elfrtida, daughter of Ordgar, Duke of Devon,
had for her beauty...

    1

    So I told him—Look,
    You count on Ethelwulf.
    Look, I said: my
    Comely person and my
    Exercise of arms.

    A fair accession
    Of land, he said,
    And it content thee.

    That's what he said.
    And I said—Look,
    You count on Ethelwulf.

    2

    The King himself
    Would have her
    In his sheets!

    Ordgar, senile
    And infirm, I
    Tricked him easily.

    But now? They
    Hasten here under
    Color of hunting.

    She ornaments herself.

3

And I must pass
Through the
Forest of Werwell.

And at night.
And alone.

To be set upon by
Desperate men.

To name her name.

Variations on a Theme by Horace

HYMNS

i
Ten times
Eleven years

ii
(the proper
cycle), may

SONGS

i
Just a week ago,
Remember? When you

ii
When you just a
Week ago, remember

GAMES

i
If indirection, certainly; if accidental, rule
The important thing of course is mental attitude

Lethal capability in highly secret fields

ii
Built a tragic theory out of physics

Winds

i
A hooded Dane of royal blood
In a little boat with his hawk

Washed ashore on a foreign
Coast in a storm

ii
An afternoon of falconry
Or murder in a private wood

A rival's madness
Or the martyrdom
of kings

Ends

i
He spoke to
Her through a convent grill

She probably
Thought
He was God

Void: fraud, duress,
The night he died

ii

The former Mrs Eugenio said
I am very much happier now

If propaganda ends
Does art begin?

Means

i
Do not use electric lights
Do not use electric chairs

Demand is over 7,000,000 kilowatts

ii
The new conductor broke his long baton
The hopless tenor coughed up blood in his beard

After Ekelöf

(for Göran Printz-Påhlson)

I broke off a branch from
A thin, young tree
Leaving an eye-knot, an eye

It watched as I thrashed
A young bride
On a coast way up in the north

I slept for five hundred years

By a great felled tree
I awoke
On a coast way up in the north

I polished a piece of the thick-veined wood
And over an eye-knot
I painted the face of a mother

Void which falls out of void...

a

Void which falls out of void, transparent,
cones, hemispheres,
fall through empy space.
Thoughtform, crescent, trajectory.

b

However relevant!
In the infinite freedom I can
keep back, give
my notes resilience, in relation
to each other, to my whole body, which also
falls in infinity through empty space:
e.g.
Charlie Parker's solo in *Night in Tunisia* on May 15th 1953.

c

The flight of sentimentality through empty space.
Through its elliptical hole
an heraldic blackbird's
black wings, yellow beak, round eyes, with the yellow
ring, which defines its inner empty
space.

*Translated from the Swedish of Göran Sonnevi
with Göran Printz-Påhlson*

August

1

The stones are hot.
The cattle are lowing.
The long-clothed infants flutter down
with a drop of milk in their mouths.
The smoke billows.
Dense pleated smoke
or the thin flesh
which rises still,
smoke from unused honey
or smoke from fires in trees.
It rises,
it brings down the subterraneans.

2

Girls and dogs
sleep in the grass
Life is
a heartbeat
from my own
              The burning cattle
with tonsured skulls
have come home
to their quivering stable.

3

Today I see that my daughter
is higher, greater
than I, and completed… Her
hard Kaiser head encircles me and carries
me and helps me. Silently
we speak
in each other and then
she paves the dead ones.
        She comes towards me in her Kaiser skirt.

From the crib of the road
in a dust cloud of sleeping crickets
her large blue eyes are watching
how the realm of day binds its book.
        She hungers after herself.

*Translated from the Swedish of Lars Norén
with Göran Printz-Påhlson*

Dunwich: Winter Visit Alone

(For Diana)

*"There is presence in what is missing; there is
history in there being so little…"*
                                        Henry James

Young & younger, we were married here
Where cliffs fall into the sea
And most of the village has
Disappeared, drowning in its leas.
I have not loved you less for that.

And if it is chastening to know
That fishermen catch
Their nets on the bell-towers,
Sunken and singing,
I have not loved you less for that,

Even though I have not loved you
As I might have, if, merchant
Or seaman, I had come here with you
To a safe coast in a good time.
No, I have not loved you less for that.

And knowing well the presences here
From the start, and of absence,
Of history alive, still, in so little,
We face the tides and erosions.
And I will not love you less for that.

No, I will not love you less for that.

Once for English Music

1

This, this is marvelous,
    this is simply too good—
I am their song, Jeremiah!
    Elgar on The Folk.

And I have worked for forty years
    and Providence denies
Me hearing of my work. So I submit:
    God is against it,

Against art. And I have worked
    for forty years and
Providence denies. And Strauss (R.),
    1905: I drink

To the welfare of the first
    English progressive.
And Gerontius: pray for me, my friends,
    who have no strength to pray.

2

And who would not put out—with his mother
Or his Queen—the night light,

Toothbrush, bathrobe and condom,
Run the bath, switch on the stereo,

Plug in the fire, and wait for time
To reverse, wait for a prince to rise

from the dead & conduct his affairs?
Neither you nor I, neither mine nor yours.

3

There in the James Gunn portrait,
There, almost, in the Beecham life—

Delius who wasn't really English,
Delius who got around:

Dying, did he summon in his cripple's dream
A syphilitic and promiscuous librettist

(In a summer garden, or on hearing the
First cuckoo in Spring)?

He would compose.
He would have his way with words.

4

During the performance
    of an overture, said Shaw,
By one of the minor Bachs,
    I was annoyed
By what I took to be the jingling
    of a bell-wire somewhere.
But it was Dr. Parry. Playing the
    cembalo part ... on a
Decrepit harpsichord.

5

Fluctuating sevenths,
    fluctuating thirds.
I'll play it on my flute
    the way it sounds.

In Surrey, in Sussex,
    airs against the harmon-
Izing organist from
    Worthing....

For Why Do The Roses?
    Because we sing enchanted.
Because we chant
    and sing.

59 Lines Assembled Quickly
Sitting on a Wall Near the Reconstruction
of the Lady Juliana's Cell

Heavily   heavily
hidden away—

the door is
barred & barred   and

singing
veni creator

spiritus "a service
of enclosure"

& the cell
is consecrated

and the door
is barred   and

singing
veni creator

spiritus you have
a window on

the church you have
a window on

the world
and appearances

and revel-
lations   visions!

"showings"
to a soul *that*

cowde
no letter: cowde—

could, cloud
no cloud or cold

unknowing sin
is what

there loud? or
quiet sin is what

behoved? or is
behovable

il convient que
le péché

existe: le péché is
serviceable

what is
an anchorhold what is

an anchoress
the Lady Juliana's

one re-
corded visit from the

frenzied Margerie Kempe
as praise

& praise & gesture
I prefer

to Juliana's
Kemp's

the *other* Kemp's
Will Kemp's

who Morris-danced
from London

days   on days
from London

Kemp's who
lept!   immortally

this Norwich wall

26 June 1381/1977

I – North Walsham: The Fields

And he, Despenser, tried to keep hold
Of the dyer's head

As the crowd of them, gawkers
& priests, tinkers & tailors & wastrels

(Gentry too, thinking already: *reredos!*
A gift for him, a

Presentiment) lurched along
With the horsecart off to the place

Of undoing, Lidster's undoing who'd heard—
Who'd heard of *The Kynges*

Son who'd paye for al,
The mullere who'd ygrounde smal—but

Was paying himself,
Tied by a foot with the same rope

That they'd hang him with, after
The drawing. And he

Henry Despenser, the Bishop "Lespenser"—
miles amatus, boni pastoris mens,

For so it says on his brass—
Hopping behind the cart like a toad,

The cart they dragged the dyer behind
For that was the law:

To be dragged to the place of undoing.
This, however, was extra:

The Bishop himself coddling your head
In his skirts

And you "The King of the Commons,"
"The Idol of Norfolk"

Whose bell had been rung
By Ball and Tyler and Straw. Oh

This dispenser of justice was special,
sui generis the man who

Had caught you, tried you, confessed you,
The man who would hang you,

See you in quarters, one for each of
The earth's: hopping

Behind the cart like a toad…
And reaching out for your head   which

Aoi!   he'd drop on a cobble a cobble
A cobble and there

Then catch it up again, mother it back
In his apron, your head

Like an apple or melon or globe. Where,
Where did you travel, where

Did you think you could go—
The two of you, then, staff, of one, life?

II – St. Luke's Chapel, Norwich Cathedral

We look at the reredos, the retables.
Of course the "subject"

Is "Christ." But the blood & the power
That steadied the hand

And shook the knees and the wits of the
Master from Norwich—*that*

Was the blood and the power of Dyer
And Bishop, of Lidster

And Henry Despenser. Behind me somebody
Mumbles the word *chiliastic*.

His fellow-tourist says, looking hard: *it's
Absolutely fantastic!*

The five panels escaped the smashing
Of Cromwell. The five

Scenes from the Passion here are restored.
And we may embrace

The arcana, study
The photomicrographic specifics:

A patient lady explains: *malachite,
Azurite*: And the head of Christ is restored!

The rotten wood is restored: the order
Is restored. *Israelite,*

Trotskyite. Edmund Burke said of the famous
Rhyme: it rhymes! And also: a sapient

Maxim: *When Adam delved and Eve span, who
Was then the gentle man?*

Nobody knows what Lidster said, but that's
What he heard: *The Kynges son schal*

Paye for al
The mullere hath ygrounde smal—and

Paid it himself,
Tied by a foot with the same rope

They'd etcetera. Spin:
The painting and the restoration

Are brilliantly done. Delve: the revolt
Alas was untimely—even Engels

Would say so—and Henry Despenser's work
Was brilliantly done—

And us with our heads still on our necks?
With books in our laps,

Stupid or giddy, gawking—
Us with the eyes still in their sockets

And tongues still in our mouths—
Where do we travel, where

Do we think we can go—
All of us now, staff, of one, life?

Brandon, Breckland: The Flint Knappers

(After a chapter in Julian Tennyson's Suffolk Scene*)*

The Forestry Commission was about to plant
the Breckland on the day young Julian Tennyson

visited the Edwardses, last knappers of Brandon.
Because some tribes in Central Africa

hadn't heard about percussion caps
there still was business for the craftsmen

that supplied the flint for Wellington
and watched the plovers & the curlews dip at home.

Alien, the Breckland seemed as sinister & desolate
to Tennyson as 1938, the stark flint cottages

all shining darkly in reflecting pools
of stone and dusty sorrel, riding in the ragwort

and the bugloss, or jutting out of bracken,
heather, thin brown grass.

Wheatears, stonechats, whinchats, pipits—
all in the same still air—

and Julian, once a Suffolk countryman's Huck Finn,
feeling terrors coming on him

now at twenty-three, feeling *loosed in some
primeval, flat and limitless arena—*

leagues and leagues and leagues of it, he wrote,
severed from the rest of England.

Brandon on the Little Ouse was a relief from that,
though still in Breckland.

Malting, watermeadows, fine old bridge—
as lovely a corner as any I have found in Suffolk.

The elder Edwards, coughing, takes him
in his workshop, shuts the door, and points:

topstone, wallstone, floorstone chips
from Lingheath Common quarry, ornaments & tinders,

flints for muskets, carbines, pistols—
quartered first, then flaked and knapped with

pointed hammer on a flattened rod of iron.
When the headmen learn about percussion caps

the show's all over, Edwards said.
And anyway we've not got one apprentice

and the quarrier's retired. It would die with him,
his art, these mysteries of Breckland.

Meanwhile Tennyson looks on amazed
as Edwards bevels edges, hammers, hammers, talks:

I did it on the radio into a microphone, I
did it on the BBC before the news.

There are reports. Off in Central Africa
sprawls a man who feels of a sudden loosed in some

primeval flat and limitless arena—
leagues and leagues and leagues of it, he thinks

in his delirium. There is a flight of birds.
On Berner's green: an Air Ministry bombing-ground;

here the Forestry Commission will plant firs.
Badgers and foxes, jays and crows

will populate the land the curlews flee, *and when
the Old Guard fell before great Wellington*

England sang the knappers of the Brandon flints!
It is the year of Munich. Tennyson will die

in Burma from a piece of shrapnel the size of any
smallish hag-stone he'd have found

among discarded chips on Edwards' dusty floor
and which his copy of George Borrow

pressing pages from a manuscript of *In Memoriam*
will not deflect. Reflected in his book,

an Indian summer. Ice will one day lift
the Blaxhall Stone itself as far as Brandon moor.

Words for Sir Thomas Browne

I

If melancholy is a sadness with no reasonable cause,
your son Tom's death at sea produced in you a grief

and not a melancholy. You would define, define again,
whose testimony helped convict, in 1655,

two witches in the court of Matthew Hale. Gentle man,
they hung on Suffolk gallows till they died.

You bore no kind of malice towards them, either one,
and you studied to avoid all controversy always.

But if no witches did the Devil's work, it followed
that no works were done among us by the Spirits,

and from that, no doubt "obliquely," that the hierarchy
of creation would collapse & neither New Philosophy

nor love could save the soul of your young Tom
who on his ship read & praised the pagans *whose noble*

straynes, you thought, may well affect a generous mind.
Amazed at those audacities, which durst be nothing,

and return into their Chaos once again, you recommended
orthodoxy and you testified for Matthew Hale.

II

Death was occupation and preoccupation both in Norwich
where you practiced medicine, exploded vulgar errors,

contemplated cinerary urns. You did not *secretly implore*
& wish for plagues, rejoyce at famines, or revolve

ephemerides in expectation of malignant aspects & eclipses
like certain others of your trade. Your prayers

went with the husbandmans, desiring *everything in proper
season, that neither men nor times be out of temper.*

But they were deeply & profoundly out of temper, the men
and times in your extraordinary time. New Science

studied to discern the cause and was itself part cause
and part effect. Love got on with its peculiar,

frail, sublunary affairs: and though you'd be *content that
we might procreate like trees without conjunction,*

husbands awkwardly attended to their husbandry, and you
yourself begot a dozen saplings. Of the seven who survived,

Edward was the firstborn and the doctor, but Tom was your
particular delight—& like to make, you thought, at once

a navigator & a scholar on that ship of Captain Brookes—
and like to take the draughts of all things strange.

III

Pythagoras and Lucan, Epicurus too: he took the draughts
of these and dwelt on noble suicides, on transmigrations,

and on souls that dwelt in circuits of the moon or souls
eternally annihilated in eternal night.

Audacious draughts: they'd make a generous mind so drunk
it might conceive itself invaded by the speech of Vulteius

and urge, in some engagement where a Netherlandish Pompey
stole the victory & then prevented honorable escape,

the sober Roman medicine you feared. How did Thomas die?
If he fell upon his sword, or, lost to Admiral Kempthorne,

lit a powder keg and blew his ship to kingdom come,
we never heard. If some malefic doctor set about to loose

a plague, or grinning crones beside a rocky coast at dawn
spun almanacks and made a storm, you never said.

You did your work: you sought to cure the ill & comforted
the dying, you strangled mice and chickens on your

kitchen scales to see *if weight increaseth when the vital
spirits flee,* you demonstrated that the elephant

indeed has joints, that beavers *do not ever in extremity
bite off their stones,* that no bear brings her

young into the world *informus and unshapen* to fashion them
by licking with her tongue, that Eve & Adam had no navels

and that Jesus wore (a Nazerite by birth) short hair.
Often you returned to your initial, fundamental ground:

Whatever impulse be unlocked by Lucan's strains, whatever
operation be insinuated in us when, Satanic,

we're inhabited by arguments which say *necessity* or *chance*
or *fate*, a lucid sense of order could, you thought,

when mixed in some alembic with humility & grace, explain
and purge away (though witches must, alas, be hanged).

IV

*As though the soul of one man passed into another,
opinions, after certain revolutions, do find men & minds*

like those that first begat them.

                                     Staring fixedly at Tom's
last letter in your hand, thinking of that trial where

one alleged his chimney had been cursed & yet another that
his cart had been bewitched and also all his geese,

you well might suddenly embrace that sweet & generous heresy
that tempted you when you were young: that all are saved—

yourself & Tom, those witches in the court of Matthew Hale,
Epicurus, Lucan & Pythagoras, cruel doctors who revolve

ephemerides, husbands who attend to husbandry, sons and
daughters, brothers aunts & sisters, wives.

And yet you said: *God saves whom he will...*
and thought the wretched women damned at Edmund's bury.

And thought you heard Tom's ship explode at sea.

Lines for the Gentlemen

I

1667. And on Landguard beach, 1000 Dutch.
That was the last invasion.
Afterwards, 1753–66,
Governor Thicknesse, thank you, defending, sir.
(And plenty of out-of-work sailors)

II

And as with piracy, there's honour in it.
And not just honour among thieves —
A rising class will not, they'd tell you,
be put down. Custom?
              Brandy! tea, wool, rum,
just name it—
So the word gets round. Someone's
had the pox, someone's
had the plague. All's free trade
at certain cottages where rumoured illnesses
or rumoured ghosts
keep all but customers away—

Laces for a lady; letters for a spy
And watch the wall, my darling, while the
  Gentlemen go by.

III

This one watched the wall; that one
closed his eyes.
The headless gunner walked on the embankment.

A crescent moon rose smartly from behind
the nasty gibbet. There are
voices in the back room of The Crown—

and Mr Plummer, MP from Appleby,
speaking in the House
and saying ALL IMPROVEMENT OF THE LAND

HAS BEEN SUSPENDED
while the Parson whispers to his wife
the wages of gin

for our duties
and hides the three enormous tubs
beneath the altar cloth.

4,000,000 gallons of booze are flowing
into England! (Three slow
cutters chasing one fast swipe.)

The publican
has put the spotsmen all to sleep.
Bright lights are flashing

down the Orwell and the Alde.

More Lines for the Gentlemen

(for L.M., age 5)

i

Thicknesse summons from obscurity
the young Gainsborough

to his Landguard Fort—
the Future's in their hands!

Like muddy Primaveras, there emerge
from busy tidal harbor into history, apotheosis:

Chesterfield and Mrs. Siddons
Pitt & Burke & Clive—

Also, though not on anybody's canvas,
not on anybody's list of invitations,

John Pixley Thomas Fidget Black George
Nichols poor Will Laud

& all
the merry rest of them—

smugglers

ii

The Rev. Richard Cobbold, Rector of Wortham and Rural Dean, writes
of Margaret Catchpole's early days:

*Who has not seen the healthy face of childhood in those ever-interesting years
when activity commences? And what philanthropist, delighting in scenes of
genuine simplicity and nature, could fail to admire the ruddy glow of youth,
and the elastic step of confidence, with which the young female peasant bounds
to meet a parent or a brother at the welcome hour of noon....*

My youngest female child, genuinely simple,
ruddy in the glow of youth,
elastic of step, confident, bounding to meet

her male parent at the welcome hour of noon,
gets it wrong. She tells her friend,
bounding with philanthropic step behind her:

My dad's writing a book about snuggling.

iii

FAMOUS SNUGGLERS ON THE SUFFOLK COAST

On Harwich: Mr. Arnott, Master of Rivers*: It was even considered dangerous to sail across the harbour after dark for fear of being set upon by snugglers.*

My Youngest Daughter: Running Toward an English Village Church

Sunday, then. In Trumpington. And nearby bells.
My daughter runs among the village graves
this foggy January morning of her early youth
as I lie late in bed
and watch her from my window.

I know she holds her breath.
Superstitious, she'll hold it till she passes by
the final marker near the door & disappears inside.
If you breathe in cemeteries
you inhale evil spirits!
What do you inhale when you breathe in stony
churches or in bedrooms where you wake alone
and realize you cannot tell
your child's superstition from her faith?

Beyond the church, a village green, a meadow,
the pleasures and the picnics
of next spring. I tell her
not to hold her breath in graveyards.
Watching her red coat become a gaudy blur
against the brilliant hoarfrost,
I realize I'm holding mine.

Mark Twain in the Fens

1

Not the trip of 1872
when fame first fanned an Anglophilia
and glory burst from every side
upon him—
And not the trip of 1879
when he howled for *real coffee,*
corn bread, good roast beef
with taste to it.

The last trip; the exile & the debts.

Thish-yer Smiley had a yeller
one-eyed cow that didn't have no tail...
At Brandon Creek, Ship Inn.
They bring him real coffee, good
roast beef with taste to it.

2

      Recently got up
by him as Joan of Arc,
his eldest daughter once had fled
the Bryn Mawr auditorium—
meningitis all but creeping
up her spine—

He told them all a tingler,
having sworn to her he wouldn't,
called *The Golden Arm.*

Death made real by hers?
and deathless tales
a part of blame? *My fault, my fault—*
And this: *I'll pay*

though still he dreams each night
about his miracle-working
machine, the Paige Typesetter,
his Dark Angel of print.

3

*Thish-yer Smiley had a yeller
one-eyed cow that didn't have no tail…*

No one writes it down
or sets it up in type. It is the last
he is going to tell.

It is all over with him. It's
begun. All night long
he tells and tells and tells.

Paul Verlaine in Lincolnshire

I

For a while he had that famous friendship.
But what's inspired debauchery
and manic vision
to illuminations from the English hymnal?
Keble's stanzas? Wesley's? Stanzas
by good Bishop Ken?
Ô mon Dieu, vous m'avez blessé d'amour.

For indulgence, there was Tennyson.
He walked to Boston from the grammar school
in Stickney to confess.

II

And wrote *Sagesse* there in Lincolnshire.
And went to chapel,
and taught the ugly boys finesse.
He had been condemned to death,
he boasted, in the Siege
of Paris…
        Colonel Grantham and
the credulous headmaster
listened to the story
of his clever rescue by Thiers....

Even in the hands of Debussy, Fauré,
the Catholic *lied* Verlainian would sing
the strangest nonconformist airs.

Ô mon Dieu, vous m'avez blessé d'amour.

III

And to proper Mallarmé he wrote
about the absinthe: *I'd still take it
with sugar....*
The school record books
do not suggest
that he excelled at rugger.

O there were many rhymes—
But he was on his best behavior,
pious, calm, bourgeois.
The peaceful English countryside
acted on his conscience
like a rudder.

Ô mon Dieu, vous m'avez, blessé d'amour.

You Measure John

for Diana, at work in the Fitzwilliam

For posterity you measure John.
For the catalogue
you measure with a tape
his works
and recognize yourself as woman
among women
in the life of this man John, his death.

You measure for the catalogue
the pictures
and their frames
thinking of the others
measuring his need
measuring his pride (who could not
please himself)
measuring his gypsy caravans of children
as he went away to paint, badly,
the famous and the rich.

No, you do not like Augustus John.
Measuring the thickness
of a new biography you offer me
I think—
not. You tell it simply
and with no embellishments yourself.
It is an old story:
some man damages the lives of women
who would love him.
There are various excuses.
One is art.

On the Death of Benjamin Britten

Operas! A feast for burghers, said Adorno.
And of your work: The apotheosis
Of meagerness, a kind of fast. That's
A cruel case against you
And it may have weight, in time.
But let's call meagerness
Economy today
And call the bourgeoisie the people
Who like me have (barely) what it costs
To listen and who like to hear
These songs, but who will pay a price.
Economies of living soon enough
Make meager even music of the spheres!
To be of use, you said.
Directly and deliberately I write
For human beings. And not
Posterity—for which the general outlook
Isn't very bright.

A tenor mourns.
And you lie down in Aldeburgh
One last time. But you have work to do
In spite of what the two of us have said.
A tenor sings. When you
Get out there over the horizon
This December morning with the likes
Of Peter Grimes,
Row your shining boat ashore
And be extravagant in song:
Leave economy to the ungrateful living
Who will need it, whose Justice
And whose History have multiplied unendingly
Expenses by Apotheoses by Sublimes.

An East Anglian Poem

1

Materials of Bronze and of Iron—

      linch-pins and chariot wheels, nave-bands
and terret-rings: harness mounts, fittings, and
bridle-bits: also a sword, an axe: also a
golden torc

            but the soils
            are acid here

            and it rains

Often there's only the mark of a tool on a bone
Often there's nothing at all

2

They hearded oxen and sheep   They hunted the deer
They made a simple pottery, spun yarn   They scratched
In the earth to little effect
                      They were afraid
     of him

     here, with his armor

              thigh and skull unearthed
                    beside the jawbone of his horse

Afraid of him who
     feared these others, Belgae,
speaking Celtic too, but building oppida, advancing,
turning sod with coulters and with broad-bladed ploughs.

       (Ceasar thought them civilized—
          which meant familiar

    They minted coins

They made war on a sophisticated scale)

3

Sub Pellibus:

    Rectangular tents in orderly lines
      and round the camp a ditch.
    Palisade stakes. Rows of javelins
      with soft iron shanks, the semi-
    cylindrical shields

            Second Augusta here—
    with auxilia: archers and slingers,
               mercenary Gauls.

He saw them on parade:

            their elegant horses, their leathers
        studded with gilt, their silvered pendants and
    the black niello inlay of their fittings
      and their rings

            their helmets made an apparition
    of the face: apertures for eyes. Their
jerkins were embroidered, their yellow plumes and
      scarlet banners sailed in the wind.

So they'd propitiate their gods.

He saw them on parade:

      to his north and east
  the boundary was the sea
      iron pikes were driven
in the Waveney and Yare

                    to his west the fenlands
          forest to the south
                    and south as well
          between the trees and fens
                    at Wandlebury here
          along a narrow belt of chalk
                    no more than eight
          miles wide

                              his ramparts rose

                    (where certain grave-goods lie)

4

Within his hornworks
Behind his stone and timber walls
Below his towers and beneath his ample crop

          these early dead

                    (he saw the Trinovantes destroyed
                    who later saw Caratacus in chains)

          their armlets and their
          toe-rings still adorn. Bronze
          bowls, amphorae, still provide.

          …and magic tokens there
          and writings there corrupted.
          With all their stolen coins,
          A carnyx there to play.

          And stood up in the marshes many days.
          Nor cried for meat.
          Nor longed for any cup.

Consider what they were before
that men could suffer labor.

And feed upon the roots and barks of trees.

5

Before him and unknown to him and
southward came the stones: dolerite-blue
with tiny bits of felspar. From the Mt. Prescelly
outcrops—Carn Meini, Foel Trigarn

        "Lord and you must climb the holy peak"

Before him and unknown to him
    the first charioteers.
        Before him, the first tamer of horses.

    He saw the hare run
    toward the sun, the

    mistletoe and sickle
    in the tree

    From the woods and the bogs
    they began to assemble

After the flat-bottom boats in the shallows of Mona

6

After the incantations and the libations
After the auguries in the grove of the dishonored queen
After the spectral bride at the mouth of the Thames

    Did the tethered swans fly above him?
    Did the deer follow behind?

And after the pounding of magic into the swords?

From the confiscated lands
From the Calendar of Rites
From the Forward Policy of Rome

From the open hands of
>   frightened and obsequious client-kings
From the pride of the Legatus
From the procurator's greed

>   From the Divine House of Tiberius Claudius
>   His octastyle temple and His Name
>   NUMEN AUGUSTI
>   From the hands of the Goddess of Death

The tethered swans flew above him
And the deer followed behind

Epilogue from a New Home:

(For Toby Barkan)

There's a plague pit
        just to the edge of the village.
Above it, now mostly covered with grass,
        a runway for B-17s: American
Pilots back from industrial targets. Tribes
        gathered under my window;
They'd sack an imperial town: I'll wave
        to my wife at the end of the Roman road.

At night I said
        (the odd smell of the house recalling home)
"My father sits up in his grave.
        I'm too unstrung to love you now. Look:
Children play in the garden with bones."

Enclosed within a boundary of stones
        they died in isolation. All of us have
Colds; we visit the parish church and read: "Names.
        The numbers of persons who died of bubonic plague."
Grey-stone cottages across the road,
        a stream at the end of the churchyard,
Giant harvesters working the mechanized farms…

Yesterday I walked to see the black,
        malignant huts that held the bombs.
After the war, nobody tore them down. Some
        are full of hay. Mechanics counted, standing
There, the number of planes that returned. I don't
        understand the work men did in the fields, or do.
I don't know the names of the crops. I don't
        know the uses of gears.
A church has grown on every hill like a tree.

Green on green: texture, shade, & shadows:
        opening out, folding in, surrounding.

Before the planes, someone counted ships: counted
        once that ancient one across the Deben
Where, from Woodbridge, you can almost see the site
        where his retainers set about to bury it,
A cenotaph, a king's.

Cynouai says: "I don't like my name. I won't have
        a name and I'll just be a girl."
Laura, three and deferential, understands. I open
        a bottle of wine.

A whir of looms where wool was wealth:
        (*nidings voerk, nidings voerk*) the baths long
Drained, the polyglot army long before withdrawn.
        If the Trinovantian coins & the legionary oaths,
If the pentatonic lyre in the Royal Ship
        prefigure here a merchant—*upon his head*
A Flaundrish bever hat—,
        is that more odd
        than that my children's rhyme recalls
The plague, the unattended fields & the dissipation
        of the feudal claims, or that the final
Metamorphosis of Anna's luck should find its
        imagery—like Christ's—in bas-reliefs
Depicting animals domesticated by domesticating
        Saxon heirs?

We picnic by these graves, these strata of
        the dead: Celtic, Roman, Viking, English—
All of them killers, all of them dead, they'd moralize
        on one another's end. Christian to pagan, power
To power, and I am also implicated here: the woodwose
        in the spandrels of a door lifts up his club,
A voice begins to speak of Fifteen Signs....

Ah, Toby Barkan,
        this is not the poem you asked me for.
Waiting for the Wickham Market train a year ago I
        sat near Liverpool Street and wrote down notes:
About your early marriage and the joy of it,
        about the way it lasted—all that joy:

About a painting left unfinished for a year,
        a painter saying that he wanted more
From life that art—
        more than just to be competent:
Meaning that he wanted you instead,
        and his son, my oldest friend,
And his son's wife,
        and his son's son and his daughter....

And meaning, I suppose,
        that competence is dangerous and deceptive,
Meaning that he'd quit:
        before he tricked himself, before he'd
Grown so old he'd suffer for it all.

And I wrote down notes about his
        playfulness, his pranks,
His driving you through fog—
        a badly marked provincial road—
Looking for something, he didn't know what,
        and sinking the car to the hubcaps,
And how you saw it then:
        the spring fields, the splendor.

I never wrote that poem.
        I wrote down words—none of them mine—
That ought to count for more:
        the Russian *Zhizneradostny*,
Which isn't "cheerful" or "joyous,"
        but even better: "life-glad."
From Brecht I wrote down *Freundlichkeit*,
        from Chaucer: *Gentilesse*.

Ah, Toby, what a thing to ask me.
        To write a poem about your husband,
Dead from cancer, whom I never really knew.
        And you were perfectly serious,
Wondering: couldn't I catch something
        of his life?

You'd tell me stories, give me the details:
>for he was life-glad and gentle,
He was kind…

In a hall at Aldeburgh an attentive audience is
>momentarily distracted by the jet (American—
The base hasn't moved very far) which flies above them
>as they listen to a song by Britten
Or by Gustav Holst. Where Thomas Hardy prayed
>(dismaying Clodd, his scientific friend),
Where George Crabbe's father preached,
>is space, is history made soluble in art,
A good man's life made durable? Cynouai is bored,
>Laura is tired. As the plane approaches,
Both of them look up. If they could understand;
>if I could let them know.

Oh, I remember you that day: the terror in
>your face, the irony and love. And I remember
What you wanted me to do. That ancient charge: to
>read whatever evidence in lives or lies appears,
In stones or bells—transform, transfigure then whatever
>comedy, catastrophe or crime, and thus
Return the earth, thus redeem the time. And this:
>To leave it all alone (unspoken always: look, I have
This moment and this place): *Cum on, cum on my owyn*
>*Swet chyld; goo we hom and take owr rest…*
Sing we to the oldest harpe, and playe … Old friend,
>old debt: I'm welcoming at last your presence now.
I'm but half oriented here. I'm digging down.

Part III

Poems 1975–1980 (2)

Double Invocation
as a Prologue to a Miscellany of Poems Mostly Written in East Anglia

i

…dRex, dregs, up & out
of the past
by the golden spurs

why not? & drags
him out from under
the bridge

from out of his grave
his marbles intact
and his relics in France

undRex, Edmund Rex
commander Rex
commando and King

and saint! all man
all mundo, myth
and sick of it too

bones in a basket
Abbo's Rex, Ailwin's Rex
and the tourist's:

this is the place
and this is
I truly apologize

only a space I must
clear to begin
and ask for your help

too looming a figure
I know it
but how could I

possibly choose
anyone else
for a guide without

losing my way? Edmund
King and Martyr,
Edmund, King of the bean?

ii

A word about Danes is also in order
to make a beginning
to get under way, but who

would put in a word, a good word
for the Danes?
Barbarous heathens you'd say

with curious names like Ubba
& Hingwar & Sweyn
the patricide killer of Blodrand

Sweyn, whose heir was Cnut—I've
spelled it correctly—
Cnut was a King and a Christian

to moot a point.
But I don't know about Danes.
Once I had an au pair

and she was a Dane.
I don't think she was a Christian—
large and marvelous tits

I kissed them once in a car
being drunk
though I never saw her Cnut

and one of my closest friends
is a Swede
which is almost a Dane

with a name like Ubba or Sweyn.
Ulfkettle may have com-
manded the army against them in 869.

That would have been against Hingwar.
Did Turchil stand against Sweyn?
I don't know very much about Danes

but O what a lovely girl, my friend,
a calamitous coast,
the wuthering troubles in store!

The Fen Birds' Cry

i

Would you take a caul
along to the sea
it prevents drowning

It shines at birth
prevents
your ship from sinking

On heads of the lucky
a membrane
it makes the solicitor grave

Endows with gift of argument
brings wealth
or would you hold

Hard to the hands of the dead.

ii

Would you hold hard to the hands
of the dead
a minute a minute a minute

Or take from the forehead a florin
there where the handywoman
put it the corpse money the florin

Would you have no child for a year
would you take
a caul along to the sea

Prevent drowning prevent
a ship from sinking & make a solicitor
grave would you hold

Hard to the hands of the dead.

Evening Song

Evening: and we
    wait for a train to pass
And my daughter
    says she sees the
Guard's van
    coming round the bend
A quarter of a mile
    or so away.

You mean
    the caboose…
I say & she looks happily
    and firmly
At the guard's van
    and pulls
At white cow parsley
    by the fence at the edge
Of the tracks
    that William Carlos
Williams
    in America called
Queen Anne's
    Lace. There's nothing
Royal at all
    about the stuff in Suffolk.

Evening. Laura pulls at
    cow parsley: we
Await the rolling guard's van.
    We live here.
Somewhere in Ohio
    the lantern on the back
Of the world's
    reddest last caboose
Vanishes
    down singing rails
Into the darkness
    of my
        childhood.

Two Ladies

I

So many incorrupt bodies, such
corrupting times!
Edmund to and fro for years,

inspected, found intact,
unburied & unbothered & unblemished.
And then, then these ladies,

these incorruptible ladies
like Etheldreda Queen & Sainted Audrey.
Earlier than Edmund even

wearing round her neck a fabled string
of beads that purpled flesh
into a fatal tumor that she liked:

she had, she said, been vain.
Daughter of the hypothetical incumbent
of the ship at Sutton Hoo,

daughter of the priest who taught her,
touchy and untouched —
by Tondbert Prince of Fenmen and

by Ecgfrith son of Osway the Northumbrian—
she ruled, queened, twice,
and got sick of it, of royalty, and fled:

fled to Abbess Eba, solicitous and grave,
where randy Ecgfrith followed
with his louts who'd leered at her around

the smutty fire inside the great log hall.
Flowering near Ely
among fowlers, among fishermen & fogs—& bogs—

famously her pilgrim's staff took root
& that was Etheldreda's Stow.
They say in Etheldreda's Stow today, they say—

that water bubbling from her temporary grave
was Audrey's Spring: & any bauble
there that's worn around the neck's called tawdry.

II

Margery Kempe from Lynn
would howl and wail "full plenteously"
when told of mirth & pleasures

"Full boisterously" she sobbed
who was no Wycliffite or Lollard but
could censure equally

some bumpkin local reprobate or mighty
philip Repington and
greater Arundel upon his Bishop's throne.

Full plenteously, full boisterously
she'd wail: full homely, too!
She was her own Salvation Army band

and drummed and trumpeted vulgarity that
such as Chesterton would
understand to be an efficacious pastorale.

Some amanuensis took it down, our first
biography—be glad! She was:
of plenteous continual weeping by a creature

who would be the bride of Christ, a pilgrim pure
and not the failed brewer, failed
miller married to the borough chamberlain

John Kempe that she, said citizens of Lynn,
pretty clearly was. Contentious;
weird; she sailed away. The Mamelukes

and Saracens were less impressed with her
outside the Holy Sepulchre
than those who'd suffered her for weeks

on board the ship. Said one: a vexèd spirit.
Another: that she'd surfeited on wine.
A third that surely fatal illnesses came on

like that: *O put her in a heavy sea*
O put her in a little boat
without a bottom O. Thus, Amanuensis says,

had each his thoughts. At
York, at Cawood Palace, the Archbishop:
"Woman!—Why, why

Then weepest thou?" And Margery: *Sir, ye*
shall wish some day
that ye had wept as sore as I!

Verrucas

The solemn doctor, eyeing painfully
My six verrucas,
Closed the heavy office door—

Well, he said, we often find in fact
The skinman doesn't
Do much good, his acids

And his sparks, they
All come back—these warts—
And so we usually

Suggest—and you Americans
Are shocked—
(He looked behind him then)

The local witch. The what?
That's right, he said.
I drove a mile or two and found

Her house. A white witch, certainly,
She smiled a kindly smile
& smoked a caked & gnarled briar pipe.

She counted up verrucas, multiplied,
And tied her knots
In just as many strings

As she would bury, burn, or bless.
I used to use a hunk
Of steak for skin disease, she said,

The method's good. I'd slap
It on a warty cheek or sole, and that
Was that. But what with

Meat so dear and all—you'll understand
We don't use mince!—this hex'll
Work for you, all right. Three days!

She packed me hobbling off
& said a spell. I tossed a silver coin
In the bottom of her well.

Mostly Joan Poulson's Recipes, Etc.

Thomas Nashe, from Lowestoft,
Opined: a red herring
Is wholesome on a frosty morning

And nowhere are they better cured
Than at Yarmouth
And a boiled one is good

For rheumatism, too. Horatio Nelson
Hung from a rope
And gathered in the luscious pears all

Dangling fruity in the master's little garden
In North Walsham. He found
Them exceptionally ripe and to his taste.

Defoe, however, thought
The Suffolk cheese "the worst in England."
Boudicca and Cymbeline

Gorged in Colchester on oysters.
Norfolk turkeys
Marched in droves through Suffolk villages

And on to London: they took the
18th century to town.
I don't know what Tom Paine liked:

They fed him Thetford porridge.
And Laurence Washington, George's great
Great granddad

Liked the Meldon new potatoes
With his mutton—
And in Heacham Pocahontas asked John Rolfe

For corn: which she did not get.
What I like is Ipswich Almond Pudding,
Aldeburgh Sprats or

Southend Cockle Cakes.
Diana serves up Greengage Mould
And says: it's good!

Laura asks for Royston Cakes
But eats a crusty Southwold Dumpling.
Cynonuai who'd have a stately

Hen-on-nest gets potted shrimps
And frowns
But eats them anyway.

Yesterday we had Saxmundham Fourses Cake,
The day before a Damson
Pickle with our Epping Sausages.

There was a time they had here absolutely
Nothing and made nettle soup
Or tried to eat the earth itself, or stones.

After lunch we walk: past the moated
Grange in Parham which was
Once the grand estate of first the Uffords

And then the Willoughby d'Ersbys.
We pass dun cows
Which still produce the Suffolk cheese

Which we enjoy and which
Defoe did not.
And for our tea we eat a Yarmouth herring.

After the Death of Chekhov

for Bob Hass

Anton Pavlovitch has died
At Badenweiler, a spa
Where doctors had sent him,

A doctor, with his beautiful Olga.
They ship the body to Moscow
Where both of us wait at the station.

This is the difference between us:
You, with Chaliapin & Gorki,
Calm the disorderly crowd

And stick with your man: You
Go off in the proper direction
And weep at the grave of the poet,

While I get confused,
Follow a band of the Tzar's
Which is playing a march

In the cortège of a general
Killed in the Japanese War.
Or, when the two coffins arrive

At the platform together,
One in a car labeled
Oysters, and you understand in

A flash which one is Chekhov's,
This is the difference between us:
You return to your wife and honor

The dead by telling hilarious jokes
About Chaliapin and Gorki, while I am sent
To a spa in the car labeled Oysters.

Friendship

One day I do you a good turn. Then
You do me *two* good turns.
I am pleased by that & say so the next day.

You break the lead in your pencil.
I loan you mine.
You give me an expensive fountain pen.

I play you a recording of The Modern Jazz Quartet.
Though you like Milt Jackson's vibes, you
Take me to *The Ring* at Covent Garden after which

We introduce each other to our wives.
My wife teaches your wife how to cook fondues.
Your wife teaches my wife how to live.

I dedicate my book to you & you are moved.
You make a character of me in yours:
It is singled out for praise by the reviewers.

I give my mistress to your loyalest disciple.
Claiming he is bored with her, you have
The wench returned; her skills are much improved.

When I sing my secret lute song about mountains,
You take me to the mountains
In your car: You have a cabin there

Where after drinks we agree to a primitive contest.
Preparing for it, you
Scar your face grotesquely with a razor blade.

Upon return, I burn for you my manuscript.
For me you smash your files. I wreck my mother's house.
You wreck your only daughter's mind.

In the end, I write a letter saying:
I forgive you. But you do not write back.
It is now the time for silence.

For we are friends. We love each other very much.

Agape

(after the poem by César Vallejo)

I won't say anyone comes here and asks.
They haven't this afternoon
Asked me for anything much. Nothing!

Not one leper presented himself.
I haven't today
Kissed my quota of sores.

In so fine a parading of lights, I haven't
Seen a single burial flower.
Lord, Lord: I've died so little today,

I'm sorry, forgive me. Everybody goes by
But nobody asks for a thing.
Mal, mal in my hands, like a *cosa ajena*.

If you've mislaid it it's here!
Well, I've gone to the door & I've shouted.
How many doors get slammed in my face!

Something *ajeno ajeno* roots in my soul
And I don't tell you somebody comes here & asks.
Lord, Lord: I've died so little today.

Poem for Cynouai

I

With urgency and passion you argue for the lot—
every one of thirty watercolors
ranged in retrospective
which I thought to choose among.
Circumspect, I sought
negotiations. You squint your lazy eye
and wave your arm in arcs
around our geocentric circle and insist:
"We'll take them all!"

II

I am easily persuaded.
How luminous their rendering of a world
we both believe in
and can sometimes share:—
where names are properties of things
they name, where stones
are animate and wilful, trees
cry out in storms, and compulsive
repetition of the efficacious formulae
will get us each his way.

When they patched your overcompensating eye
your work began. Your starboard
hemisphere was starved for colors
and for shapes.
Suddenly a punning and holistic
gnostic, you painted
everything in sight:
your left eye flashed at cats & camels
in the clouds, while one by one
you drew them with a shrewd right hand
into a white corral.

At school they said your "problem"
was "perceptual."

III

What did you perceive,
and what did I?
I found that scattering of words
in notes. I wrote it down
two years ago and now you do not paint.
I no longer wrote. It's out
of date, we've changed.
I was going to quote Piaget
and go on to talk about perception.
Instead I went to work
and earned some money, girl.
I was going to call
you *child*.

Two years, then. We'll keep it honest
as I wander back with you
to Shelford. Bob & Earlene live in Shelford
now, Leif and Luke and Kristin.
Bob has poems in which
he whispers *child, child*.
"We'll take them all," you said,
and I said
I am easily persuaded.
We took just one.

IV

But it is altogether marvelous.
I've kept it here while
you've gone riding with your friends.
Your passion now is horses.
It feels as if you've been away two years—
two years.

Stout-hearted Moshe,
peering one-eyed through your
horse's ears, this bright Ikon that
you've left me makes me
think of William Blake's *Glad Day*.
One sad poet wrote: My
daughter's heavier. And another:
O may she be beautiful, but
not *that* beautiful. I have a friend
who's visited Ms. Yeats—
She's bald with warts! O daughters
and their bright glad days
growing beautiful or heavier or bald.
O foolish leers and Lears.

We played. And we play now, but
not so much. Our problem
was perceptual. I think we were
perhaps too Japanese:
I have it on authority
that formal speech retains
the spirit of *bushido* in Japan.
In the *Asobase-Kotaba*
we don't say: "I'm here in Shelford"
or "You're riding"
but: "I pretend to be in Shelford"
or "You play at
going riding." Nor does one say:
"I hear your father's dead,"
but this instead:
"I understand your father
has played dying."

V

When my father finished playing dying
I began.
You gave me pictures
which I held against a wound.

I wrote: "How luminous their rendering
of a world we both believe in"
and then I think you stopped believing....

For money, with a friend,
I helped to translate Lars Norén
who far away
in dark, cold Sweden wrote:

Today I see that my daughter
is higher, greater
than I, and completed... Her
hard Kaiser head encircles me & carries
me and helps me. Silently
we speak in each other—Then
she paves the dead ones.
She comes towards me in her Kaiser skirt.

How I stumbled after you with memories & books.
How far ahead you rode. How very
quickly all the books
were closed. How frightening the horses are

As you approach me on The Black Duke of Norfolk.
The Duke's Funeral Helm is low on your eyes
(I stole it for you from a golden nail
in Framlingham church).
Your Ming Dynasty jodhpurs cling to your legs,
cling to your horse's sides
(I sent for them express to Rajasthan).
Your Dalai Lama coat is zipped up tight
(I zipped it up myself).
Your green Tzarina vest divests me.
Your beady Pony Club badge is a third eye
pinned to your cheating heart.
On a velvet photograph of Princess Anne
you are riding in circles of dust.
One eye is patched, old pirate,
and the other eye is glazed.
Only the third one, the Pony Club badge,

can see me, and it stares,
fiery and triumphant.
You are riding in circles of dust.
You are riding into the eye of the Pony Club badge.

First they patched your eye
and then I saw.
My problem was perceptual.

Lars Norén concludes:
She hungers after herself....

VI

What I had wanted to say was: *red, ocher,*
orange, blue, green, violet.
What I had wanted to say was: grass, sky,
sun, moon, child, forest, sea.
I had wanted to say: *English village.*
I had wanted to say:
English village a long time ago....
What I had wanted to hear
was the music of flutes and recorders
in a summer garden—
flutes and recorders and tambourines....

What I had wanted to see was light
filtering through the trees
deep in a forest near the sea
where elves and children play together
and adults sip tea
by an enormous ornamented samovar
in solemn conversation
on the nature of the games
the elves & children play....
What I had wanted to write was
love, immortal, laughter, wings....
What I had wanted to do
was to walk forever into a vision

painted by my daughter.
I had wanted her to take me with her there.
I had wanted her
to close the door behind us....

VII

Made of blues and ochers, greens,
made of sunrise and of grass & sky & trees—
which will be the day
that you remember, child,
when I am only soul-stuff
and can no more enjoy this awkward body
which, despite its ills,
manages to do extraordinary simple things
like walk through heaths of gorse
with you before the others are awake
as the sun comes over
the edge of the earth the ships fall off of
as they tilt on their keels
and roll on the world's last wave....?

I remember a day: the rowboat rocked
in the reeds:
my father watched his line. All
the night before we had slept together
in a shack waiting for the dawn.
We didn't talk for hours. He, for once,
was beautifully distracted from
what he always called "the difficult business
of living." There was
no past, there was no future there
in those reeds...
                      we were adrift in time,
in timelessness
and no one said we must return—

nor did we sail over any edge of any earth.

Or again: near the house of my childhood
on a street called Glen Echo Drive
there was a tree, an oak,
where my father swung me in a swing—
his long thin fingers
and his firm damp palms on the small of my back
I feel still—
and my bare & grimy feet going up through the leaves!

Mosses grow between his fingers now
and along his palms.
Mosses grow in his mouth & under his arms.
When he finished playing dying
I began....
You gave me pictures
which I held against a wound.
I wrote: *How luminous their rendering as*

You came toward me saying *muzzle, poll, crest,*
withers, loins, croup, dock...
As you came saying *snaffle, whip, spurs,*
pommel, cantle, girth.

VIII

And so I try to learn new words
like any child—
I say *flank, hock, heel, hoof;*
I say *fetlock, gaskin, thigh, stifle, sheath.*
I would meet you now
according to my bond. I try to put away
this Ikon which sustained me.
I write *Equitation: Mounting & dismounting.*
Circumspect, I seek
negotiations. I wave my arms
around in frantic circles and insist:
"I'll learn them all"
while you ride off on paths

through fields of gorse and into sunsets
which are not even slightly picturesque—

While you ride off in hurricanes of dust.

—Just one time were three of us together:
father, father-son, and daughter.
We played at something, riding, painting,
poetry, or dying—it hardly matters what . . .
And at our playing
              —(while, perhaps,
someone picked a mandolin
and strangers talked about us solemnly
around an ornamental samovar
and sipped their tea)—
our lines of vision crossed
and then we started changing places painfully. . . .

The child is father of the man
but not the child the poet meant.
The child of flesh and blood
and not the ghost of former selves
is father of the man—
The Daughter on the Black Duke of Norfolk
She
is father of the man
The Daughter
Who is Higher, Greater & Completed
She
is father of the man
The Daughter on the Black Duke of Norfolk
The one who made the picture
the one who gave the gift
the one who paved the dead
the one who wore the patch
the one who was Japanese
the one who learned to ride a horse
And Hungers After Herself—

She
is father of the man
The daughter on the Black Duke of Norfolk

The one whose problem was perceptual

The one who rides away

> And the Manual says: *It is interesting to assess the progress and accuracy of the training by riding a circle on ground upon which the imprints of the horse's hoofs can be seen....*

(1974-1977)

Turns:
Toward a Provisional Poetics and a Discipline

I

The scolemayster levande was the toun
and sary of hit semed everuch one.
The smal quyt cart that covert was and hors…
to ferien his godes. To ferien his godes
quere he was boun.

The onelych thyng of combraunce (combraunce)
was the symphonye
(saf a pakke of bokes)
that he hade boghte the yere
quen he bithoght
that he wolde lerne to play.

But the zele woned (zele woned).
He neuer couthe ani scylle.

II

And so the equivalent
    (the satisfactory text.
squ'elles sont belles
    sont pas fidèles. Rough
west-midland, hwilum andgit
of andgiete: the rest is not
    a word for word defense....

III

And make him known to 14th-century men
Even when everything favors the living?
Even if we could reverse that here
I know you've read and traveled too.

So Destination or Destiny: Quere He was Boun!
And yet to introduce the antecedent place.
Restrictive clause; sense of the referent noun.
A tilted cart is a cart with an awning.

    Langland has it "keured"
    John of Mandeville "coured"
    Wycliffe "keuered"

    But "covert" in Arimathaea

Personal luggage: not the same as merchandise.
Cursor Mundi's "gudes;" Purity's "godes"

This is personal luggage / destination / travel

    Harp and pipe and symphonye

    (saf a pakke of bokes)

IV

Where dwelle ye if it tell to be?

    at the edge
        of the toun?

    at the edge
        of the toun?

Levande was.
He Levande Was The Toun.

Reason the nature of place
Reason he can praise
Reason what the good-doing doctor said

    Rx.:cart   (that covert was & hors)

Dull ache in the hip is probably gout.
Painful nodes of calcium—(neck & in the ears).
Palpitations, flutters. Stones in the gland.

   food to avoid?   Drink

      (put him in the cart)

   Rx.: bibliography
   Rx.: map

V

The metaphysicality of Hermetic thought—
Let him think o' that! (Problem is he
Still enjoys cunt...)

...instrument was ay thereafter
Al his own combraunce...

Sary of hit semed everuch one.
Torn between disgust & hope
He simply never couthe...

antiquorum aegyptiorum
oh, ... imitatus...

VI

All day long it rains. He travels
All day long. Wiping water from
His eyes: and twenty miles? and
Twenty miles? Fydlers nod & smile.

Cycles pass him. Cars pass him.
Buses full of tourists...
Dauncers & Minstrels, Drunkards
And Theeves. Whooremaisters,

Tossepottes; Maskers, Fencers
And Rogues; Cutpurses, Blasphemers
Counterfaite Egyptions . . .

Greek, Arabic, Medieval Latin,
Mis-translated, misconceived.
More than just for his disport

   who loveth daliaunce

who falleth   (o who falleth)

far behinde…

VII

That supernatural science,
That rare art should seem…

   here among
   a randy
   black-billed

   ilk

Les traductions sont comme les femmes. And time to get off of her toes. Idiomatic: toes. Lorsqu'elles sont belles. I should apologize, then: to apologize. The schoolmaster was leaving the village, and everybody seemed sorry. Simple as that. The miller lent him the cart and horse to carry his goods. Simple as that. And no particular trouble with the words. Scolemayster: 1225 in the *Life of St Katherine*. But you change the spelling, see, to conform with the dialect. Levande was: *The Destruction of Troy*, "all the Troiens lefton." But use the participial construction. Sary of hit: see the *Lay Folks Mass Book*. The city of his destination. Twenty miles off. Quite sufficient size for his effects. The only cumbersome article (save the pack of books) was: count on the medieval mind to be sympathetic. Though I come after hym with hawebake/I speke in prose and lat hym rymes make. My general principles I take from the King (and his Queen). Tha boc wendan on Englisc. Hwilum word be word. Hwilum andgit of andgiete. Swa swa ic hie geliornode. It would be idle and boring to rehearse. Here what is available. Let me simply indicate the manner. Take sulphur from Sol for the fire and with it roast Luna. From which will the word issue forth.... *If* the given appeared in a verifiable text.... *If* the given was truly equivalent.

The usual procedures are the following: (1) To ignore altogether: "make no effort to explain the fundamentals." (2) To drop apologetic footnotes: "I'm sorry, but I simply cannot understand this esoteric sort of thing." (3) To make suggestive remarks while hurrying on to something else: "*If* the given appeared in a verifiable text. *If* the given was truly equivalent." But the schoolmaster was leaving the village, and everybody seemed sorry. *Jude the Obscure*, paragraph one, a neat linguistic exercise. Written by Thomas Hardy in 1895. And such a revelation makes the art available to the vulgar. Who will abuse and discredit? *Keeper of secret wisdom, agent of revelation, vision and desire:* THIS IS THE QUESTION WE MUST ALWAYS RAISE.

Now some of the obscure, like some of the lucid, do not become proletarianized. Unlike the majority of their kind, they are not cast down from the ruling class to produce a commodity which both enslaves them and enslaves the exploited labourers with whom they are objectively allied. Perhaps they hold teaching jobs in public schools or universities; perhaps they have an inherited income. In any case, some maintain their Hermetic privilege. They are not obliged to live by their art or to produce for the open market. Such unproletarianized obscure are revolted by the demands of a commercialized market, by the vulgarity of the mass-produced commodity supplied to meet it. And revulsion ultimately tells (1) on their sex life (2) on their health.

While a relationship of cause and effect is established between obscure and lucid organizations emerging from the division of labour and the consequent dialectical evolution of social reality, such becomes, we know, increasingly separated from the actual productive function of society, from sleep. This gives us pause. "The point is that the notion of invariancy inherent by definition to the concept of the series, if applied to all parameters, leads to a uniformity of configurations that eliminates the last traces of unpredictability, of surprise." This gives us pause.

And so the system and its adherents are the villains; license, conspiracy, and nihilism are the virtues of the heroes: *or*: The system itself becomes a context for heroics; license, conspiracy, and nihilism become the crimes of the villains; acceptance of convention and austere self-discipline become the virtues of the heroes. The schoolmaster is forever an intermediary: the shape of his life is determined by the nature of society: the nature of his art seeks to determine the shape of society by administering to its nature. And intermediacy ultimately tells (1) on his sex life (2) on his health.

But make him known to 14th-century men even when everything favors the living. Reason the nature of place. Reason he can praise. Reason that he travels in a cart. With Cursor Mundi's "gudes"; with Purity's "godes." With Joseph of Arimathaea, turns: to elliptically gloss.

Double Derivation, Association, and Cliché:
from *The Great Tournament Roll of Westminster*

I

The heralds wear their tabards correctly.
Each, in his left hand, carries a wand.
Before and after the Master of Armour
enter his men: three of them carry the staves.
The mace bearer wears a yellow robe.
In right & goodly devysis of apparyl
the gentlemen ride.
The double-curving trumpets shine.

Who breaks a spear is worth the prize.

II

Or makes a forest in the halls of Blackfriars
at Ludgate whych is garneychyd wyth trees & bowes,
wyth bestes and byrds; wyth a mayden
syttyng by a kastell makyng garlonds there;
wyth men in woodwoos dress,
wyth men of armes....
    Or Richard Gibson
   busy
with artificers and labour, portages and ships:
busy with his sums and his accounts:
for what is wrought by carpenters & joyners,
karrovers & smiths...
(Who breaks a spear is worth the prize)
who breaks a schylld on shields
a saylle on sails
a sclev upon his lady's sleeves;
who can do skilfully the spleter werke,
whose spyndylles turn

Power out of parsimony, feasting
Out of famine, revels out of revelation:—
Out of slaughter, ceremony.
When the mist lifts over Bosworth.
When the mist settles on Flodden.

Who breaks a spear is worth the prize.

III

The double-curving trumpets shine:
    & cloth of gold.
The challengers pass…

Well, & the advice of Harry Seven:—
(or the Empress Wu, depending
where you are):
We'll put on elegance later.
We'll put off art.
No life of Harry the Seven
    there in the works of the Bard…
(No Li Po on Wu)
An uninteresting man? Parsimonious.

Wolsey travels in style…
       & on the Field of Cloth of Gold
  & in the halls at Ludgate a little style.…
Something neo-Burgundian
(Holy, Roman & bankrupt) illuminating
Burgkmairs in *Der Weisskunig* & *Freydal*.
Rival Maximilian's mummeries, his
dances and his masques, his
armouries & armourers the mark.
Hammermen to King, his prize; King
to hammermen: guard, for love of progeny,
the private parts!
      (My prick's bigger
than *your* prick, or Maxi's prick,
or James')

IV

       & like the Burgkmairs
these illuminations:—
where, o years ago, say twenty-two or
say about five hundred,
cousins in the summertime would
ritualize their rivalries
in sumptuous tableaux.
Someone holds a camera. Snap.
In proper costume, *Homo Ludens* wears
imagination on his sleeve.

But chronicle & contour fashion
out of Flodden nothing but the truth.
The deaths, in order & with dignity,
of every child: I remember that.

Who breaks a spear is worth the prize.

V

Who breaks a schylld on shields
    a saylle on sails
a sclev upon his lady's sleeves…
And in the north, & for the nearer rival.
Who meteth Coronall to Coronall, who beareth
a man down:—down the distance to Westminster,
down the distance in time.

For the pupil of Erasmus,
for the rival of the Eighth,
a suitcase dated Flodden full of relics.
Shipped Air France, they're scattered
at the battle of the Somme.
It intervened, the news:
it intervenes

As, at the Bankside, Henry makes
a masque at Wolsey's house and, certain
cannons being fired, the paper
wherewith one of them is stopped
does light the thatch, where being
thought at first but idle smoke,
it kindles inwardly consuming
in the end
the house
the Globe

          The first & happiest hearers of the town
          among them, one Sir Henry Wotton

Largely Fletcher's work

VI

O, largely spleter werke
that certain letters could be sent
unto the high & noble excellent Princess
the Queen of England from her dear & best beloved
Cousin Noble Cueur Loyall with knowledge of
the good and gracious fortune of the birth
of a young prince:
      & to accomplish certain
feats of arms the king (signed Henry R)
does send four knights…

   & sends to work his servant Richard Gibson
on the Revels and Accounts
& sends the children in the summertime to play
& sends the rival Scott a fatal surrogate
from Bosworth, makes an end
to *his* magnificence.

Slaughter out of ceremony, famine
out of feasting, out of power

parsimony, out of revels
revelation…

        As an axe in the spine can reveal,
     as an arrow in the eye.

Who breaks a spear is worth the prize.

VII

And what is wrought by carpenters & joyners,
by karrovers & smiths, is worth the prize;
and what is wrought by labour.
For those who play. Of alldyr pooles & paper,
whyght leed and gleew, yern hoopes of sundry
sortes; kord & roopes & naylles:—
All garneychyd at Ludgate. With
trees & bows. All garneychyd with
cloth of Gold.

           The challengers pass

And deck themselves outrageously
in capes & plumes and armour…
And out to play: making in the summertime
a world against all odds, and with
its Winter dangers.

        In a garden, old men play at chess.
        In the Summer. In the Winter, still.

Who will decorate the golden tree,
employ properly the captive giant
and the dwarf? Who will plead
his rights despite decrepitude…?

        I reach for words as in a photograph
       I reach for costumes in a trunk:

An ancient trunk (an ancient book)

    a saylle, a schylld, a sclev
    a yellow robe, a wand—

        pipes & harpes & rebecs,
        lutes & viols for a masque.

Where double-curving trumpets shine
The challengers pass.

Who breaks a spear is worth the prize.

Clarifications for Robert Jacoby
("Double Derivation...", Part IV, ll. 1–10; Part VII, ll. 1–15, 22–28)

A moment ago, Robert, I thought I was watching
    a wren, the one which nests
By my window here, fly, dipping & rising,
    across this field in Suffolk
So like the one we used to play in, in Ohio,
    when we were boys. But it was
Really something that you, Dr Jacoby, would
    be able to explain by pointing out
To me in some expensive, ophthalmological text
    the proper Latin words.

It was no wren (still less the mythological bird
    I might have tried to make it)—
But just defective vision: one of those spots
    or floating motes before the eyes
That send one finally to a specialist. Not
    a feathered or a golden bird,
Nothing coming toward me in the early evening
    mist, just a flaw, as they say,
In the eye of the beholder.

Like? in a way?
    the flaw in the printer's eye
(the typesetter's, the proof-
    reader's) that produced and then
Let stand that famous line
    in Thomas Nashe's poem about the plague,
"Brightness falls from the air,"
    when what he wrote was, thinking
Of old age and death, "Brightness
    falls from the *hair*."

I wonder if you remember all those games
    we used to play: the costumes,
All the sticks & staves, the whole complicated
    paraphernalia accumulated to suggest

Authentic weaponry and precise historical dates,
    not to mention exact geographical places,
All through August and September—the months you
    visited. You wanted then, you said,
To be an actor, and your father—a very practical
    lawyer—said he found that funny, though
I think we both intuited
    that he was secretly alarmed.

With little cause. You were destined—how obvious
    it should have been!—to be professional,
Respectable, and eminent. Still, you put in time
    and played your child's part
With skill and grace.

There is a photograph of us taken, I believe,
    in 1950. Your plumed hat (a little
Tight) sits sprightly on your head, your cape
    (cut from someone's bathrobe) hangs
Absurdly down your back, and in your hand you
    brandish the sword of the patriarch
Himself, grandfather M., Commander in Chief
    Of the United Spanish War Vets.
                            My
Plumed hat is slightly better fitting, if less
    elegant, my sword a fencing foil with
A rubber tip, my cape the prize: something from
    the almost legitimate theatre, from
My father's role in a Masonic play where he spoke,
    once each year before initiations
On some secret, adult stage, lines he practiced
    in the kitchen all the week before:
Let the jewelled box of records be opened
    and the plans for the wall by the
South west gate be examined!

The photographer, it seems, has irritated us.
    We scowl. The poses are not natural.
Someone has said Simon says stand here, look
    there, dress right, flank left;

Someone, for the record, intervenes. Or has
    James arrived? Our cousin from the
East side of Columbus who, with bicycles
    and paper routes and baseballs
Wanted you in time as badly then as I could
    want you out of it. A miniature
Adult, he looked askance at our elaborate
    rituals. He laughed outright,
Derisively. No mere chronicler, he was reality
    itself. I hated him.

Of whom I would remind myself when asking you:
    do you remember? a world of imagination,
Lovely and legitimate, uncovering, summer after
    summer, a place that we no longer go,
A field we do not enter now, a world one tries
    to speak of, one way or another,
In a poem. Robert! Had the jewelled box
    of records been opened and the plans
For the wall by the south west gate been examined,
    news: that he, not you and I, made
Without our knowledge, without our wigs and
    epaulets, with bricks he had a right
To throw, binding rules for our splendid games.

How remote it all must seem to you who joined
    him with such dispatch. One day, I
Suppose, I'll come to you in California saying
    to you frankly: cure me if you can.
Or to some other practicing your arts. Until then,
    what is there to talk about except
This book of photographs? And what they might
    have made of us, all those aunts,
Clucking at our heels, waddling onto Bosworth field
    or Flodden with their cameras. And why
They should have come, so ordinary and so mortal,
    to bring back images like this one
Turning yellow in a yellow book. Brightness fell
    from the hair

Of whom I would be worthy now, of whom I think
    about again as just outside my window
A child plays with a stick. And jumps on both feet
    imitating, since she sees it in the field
(With a stick in its beak), a wren. She enters
    the poem as she enters the field. I will
Not see her again. She goes to her world of stick
    and field and wren; I go to my world
Of poem. She does not know it, and yet she is here:
    here in the poem as surely as there
In the field, in the dull evening light, in the world
    of her imagining, where, as the mist descends,
She is a wren.

As I write that down she is leaving the field.
    She goes to her house where her
Father and mother argue incessantly, where
    her brother is sick. In the house
They are phoning a doctor. In the poem—
    because I say so,
                   because I say once more
That she enters the world of her imagining
    where, as the mist descends,
She is a wren—
    She remains in the field.

Part IV

Poems 1975–1985

On a Slip of the Tongue

"…and in my father's life at the very end of his mind…"
—Imogen Holst, BBC 3

And what was in
your father's life

at the very end
of his mind?

A sound, a sound
was in his mind

at the very end
of his life

but what was found
in his life & wound

at the very end
of his mind?

Words for Karl Wallenda

(Wallenda was the great aerialist, killed in a fall in San Juan in 1978. His most famous stunt, in one performance of which several members of his acrobatic family were killed or injured, was called 'The Pyramid.')

i

  & is   your losses
the rope   & your net

as narrow as   & catch the
these   less compulsive

lines   when they
& would   stumble

you walk it   tumble
get   past you

a family   in your arms
on it   or watch

build   them fall?
your house

upon it   & would
Karl Wallenda   you call

not of stone   your house
but of   a pyramid

their bones   & you
& yours   he Cheops

agility &   in it
will   & the priest

and would   & mason
you cut   of it too

who know
or knew the

reasons &
the seasons

the rivers
& the winds

& is
your house

as narrow as
these

lines
& would you

try to
move it on

a rope
as narrow

as these
lines

until it
falls

around you
to the

clownish
circus floor

laws of balance
all intact

but in-laws
tackless

sailing by
& fall-

ing
past you

Karl Wallenda
on all

sides

ii

& would you
leave

that fallen
house

to walk alone
one morning

in San Juan
& did you

take an easy
walk this

morning in
San Juan

& did you
lean

into the
sea breeze

with a smile
until it

stiffened for
a passage

to the
chambers of

a pyramid
that no

one saw
or had foreseen

& did you lean
Wallenda

toward it
& then

fall
& did you

fall like
Icarus

or Troy
did you fall

like Adam
did you lean

all human
out of balance

did you fall
& did you

fail to rise
upon the wind

or walk
upon the water

did you fall
& did you

slide into
the passage

in the
northern face

& pass into
the chamber

for the King
& did you

leave us
in amazement

& on ropes
as narrow

as these
lines

& with
your name

upon our lips
Wallenda

Three Around a Revolution

I – A Gift

He is the Tribune of The People,
He is Babeuf. The others speculate,

But he is Babeuf. The others
Speculate and steal. Gracchus

Out of Plutarch, he takes
The crudely fashioned knife

Made by his son from a candlestick
For his (the father's) suicide.

He hones it on his eloquent tongue.
He says, smiling enigmatically:

Here, it is yours. Do what you can.

II – Alternatives

One announces in papers:
Seeking the patronage of the rich

To further my work. For a decade
It will always be noon.

Nobody's wealth intervenes
Between freedom and time.

One in despair discharges a gun:
Nevertheless, he goes on writing

Noblesse oblige with seven balls
Of shot in his brain.

Making accurate measurements,
Another says: *Here we may build,*

Here we may bathe, here we may breathe.

III – A Letter

There must be horses, there must be women,
There must be lawsuits. There must, moreover

And eventually, be justice. There must be words.
I write down words. Are we lost in our names?

Yesterday I spoke for hours and nobody stirred.
Rapt. They cheered. I am a hero.

I said words like action, money, love, rights
And was moved to elegance, alliteration,

Saying, apropos of what I did not know,
Palfrey, palindrome, pailing, palinode, palisade.

Born 1851, Henry Demuth

Neither wife nor daughter, posterity nor poem
The shops of Soho nor the Soho whores

Could feed Prometheus's progeny
The year of his begetting.

Whose mother was called Lenchen,
Whose sister called him Frederick,

Whose father touched the pulses of the poor
And wrote, and wrote, and wrote

Would drive his taxi through the filthy
Town for years while every bell

In London rang out *Manchester* and *More*!

Bakunin in Italy

Wagner's face is still illuminated
Over Dresden in that fire I fed

And in the glow of it I see my sister
Walking through the snow beside Turgenev.

Did I spit my teeth out in the Peter-Paul
Only to release the homicidal genius

Of Nachaev? I should have been a Jesuit,
A Mason. Castrati sing the Internationale

And dance the choreography of Karl Marx.
I should have been a tenor playing

Sophie Hatzfeldt in an *opera-bouffe*
By Ferdinand Lassalle.

Zurich to London, Tzara to Trotsky

A black horsehair sofa, Lev Davidovich.
A predilection for exaggerated widow's weeds.

An oratorio by Handel, Lev Davidovich.
A gaudy-feathered peacock under glass.

A red plush chair with a gilt frame.
An enormous mahogany wardrobe.

Face of an Odessa jailer cut in crystal.
A Chrystal Palace and a Christian Prince.

Nickname, The Pen; weakness, Beauty.
Already you are old. I have just been born.

A Painter

Mark Chagall knew nothing
About dialectics.

Gaily, daily, in Vitebsk,
Cows & horses danced in the air.

Superstructure he hopelessly
Muddled with structure.

Gaily, daily, in Vitebsk,
Cows & horses danced in the air.

After October, Chagall was
Commissar of the Arts for a year…

But was dismissed: The Man
Leaping Over The City.

Daily, daily, in Vitebsk,
Icons of Lenin & Stalin objectively stare.

Alexander Kerensky at Stanford

He rose one winter from his books
To sit among the young, unrecognized.

It was 1963. It was 1917.
He sipped his coffee & was quite anonymous.

Students sat around him at their union
Talking politics: Berkeley, Mississippi.

A sun-tanned blonde whose wealthy father
Gave her all his looks and half his money

Whispered to her sun-tanned lover:
"Where is Viet Nam?"

He thought no thought of theirs.
In his carrel at the Hoover Institute

He had the urns of all his ancient enemies.
Their dust was splattered on his purple tie.

Five for Michael Anania

1 Trithemius

Orifiel reigned:
        March 15
                The first year of the world.

So, Trithemius, timid and wise.
So, Agrippa. Light!

Paid the debts at Sponheim.
Drove the lazy monks.
God's breath, good books: stone.

Vulgar speak of vulgar things.
So, Agrippa. Light!

Maximillian in my
        Cunning circle
                Trod.

2 Agrippa von Nettesheim

Nothing less than total reform
Mystical. Of the world.

Margaret of Austria, O Mirific Maid,

August, divine, and very clement chick,
I'm on the dole.

The Nobility of Women Folk—
Exalt I phrases here…
Dollars for the scholars, sweetheart; smile.

So that Franciscan calls me heretic.
So Inquisitor Savini burns his share.

Frogs' eyes. Mule piss.
Everyone's Pythagorean here.

3 PARACELSUS

All things change save one.
All things one save change.

Re-ligare means unite again.

Areopagite of Athens,
Follow *now*. Where?

The patients of the Galenians died.

And in her hand
       (the Queen's)
              I'll put a rose.
And in his hand
       (the King's)
              I'll put a golden crown.

And in the sea aboard their ship
The King he'll take his Queen.

The patients of the Galenians died.

4 NOSTRADAMUS

The curious words remain. The seer sees.
Single combat on a lawn; the bloody axe.

Out of time, he travels in it still.
Catherine de Medici knows. Henry II is warned.

The act occurs as it is seen the act occurred.

Out of time, he traveled in it still.
Catherine de Medici knew. Henry II was warned.

The curious words remained. The seer saw.
Single combat on a lawn; the bloody axe.

The act occurred as it is seen the act occurs.

5 Rosencreutz to Saint-Germain

We did not mean Brother Martin.
We did not mean 30 years war

We did not mean Huguenots
Or St. Bartholomew's Eve.

We did not mean property.
We did not mean money.

We did not mean Pope
Or the Place de la Grève.

But no more maneuvers.
All are vowed to death.

Too late. I have done all I can.

Double Sonnet on the Absence of Text:
"Symphony Mathis der Maler,"
Berlin, 1934: — Metamorphoses

I

The eschatology of Jews and Christian heretics:
Unearthly metal glows. *Schafft er nicht mehr—*
He lies among his tools.
Geh hin und bilde. Geh hin und bilde
Polyptich as polyphony. Medieval modes,
Matis: Gothardt, Neithardt. Grunewald
To historians, *der Maler.*
Father of no child though, Regina; father
Of his altarpiece at Isenheim, father
Of his torments, his tormentors,
Dying in obscurity at Halle building mills.
Geh hin und bilde. For Albricht, Luther
Or for Muntzer? *Geh hin und bilde.*
The pointing finger of an evangelic hand
Outlasts apocalypse.

II

The libretto: that's the crux, the words.
Because of that the senile Strauss would
Play *Gebrauchsmusik* for Goebbels who, while
Furtwängler's applauded by the partisans
Of Brecht or Grosz or Benn, sits
On hams beside the corpse of Wagner.
Oh that Hindemith should feel the pull
Of Matis: What's the distance, then, from
Buchenwald to Yale? *Ist, dass du
Schaffst und bildest, genug?*
Abandoned, all the words: for what
They cannot settle will be left alone.
Leaving us just where, Professor?
Contemplating cosmogonic harmonies with Kepler.
In oblivion with courage and acoustics.

At a Screening of Gance's *Napoleon*: Arts Theatre, Cambridge

In the shadow of the eastern towers of Kings
and in the Sunday-dinner darkened theater where
Lydia Keynes once danced the frozen breath away
from puffing Cambridge dons, we eat our

sandwiches between parts three and four of
Abel Gance's reconstructed, spliced-together,
silent, five-hour epic of Napoleon.
I am, said Bonaparte, *a rock thrown into space.*

We can believe it. Spinning giddily from images
of Corsica to images of storms tossed up by
the Sirocco, the Convention, and Rouget de Lisle,
we'd clutch at almost anything, even this

unfashioned rock that tumbles through the space
of an unfinished film and cries: *to make
yourself well understood, speak to people's eyes*!
Our eyes are red; we rub them in the interval

and stuff our mouths with cheese & chutney, wash
it down with Beaujolais kept cool in a thermos.
Somewhere in part two, reel seventeen or so,
beneath the guns of Admiral Hood pounding batteries

outside Toulon where Dugommier attacks the captured
port, Bonaparte assumed command. The silence
of all that exhausted us: this black & white morality
keeps its moral to itself or hasn't got one yet.

Shall we see in Antonin Artaud's Marat, or even
in Maxudian's Barras, the cruel stuff of History?
Or do we gape of mysteries of Art? (We might have
left before the Terror if we hadn't brought our

sandwiches and wine.) Abel Gance maintained that
he had made Prometheus. He said (aloud)
he'd found a cinematic style capable of Vision.
Then the markets crashed and Jolson's busy progeny

made all those early talkies sing & pay their way.
War's anachronism, said this hero of the triple screen,
tearing every city down in sight. And Gance:
All those polyvision sequences to come, you've seen.

Ahhhh! We said, watching Cinerama in the fifties,
waiting for the famous rollercoaster ride that actually
made kids throw up their popcorn. These final reels
will march us out beyond the foothills through the Alps,

the screen split into three to make us gasp:
As triptych or as trinity, *Les Mendiants de la Gloire*
will traipse behind Napoleon into Italy—
We'll never see the Empire or a sunset by the Loire.

We'll wait, like Josephine, with spots before our eyes:
those blinking phantoms a machine's already loosed,
the gangling ghosts of Robespierre, Marat,
the feminine, impassioned, & most elegant Saint-Just

Unpleasant Letter

1
Information has this day been laid
By R.L. Waters

Of the Cambridgeshire Constabulary
Who states that you—

That *you* on 28.4.77
Did at Sidgwick Avenue in the said

City during the hours of darkness
Cause a pedal cycle

To be on the road when it did not
Carry (a) one bright lamp which showed

White light to the front
And (b) one bright lamp which showed

Red light to the rear
Visible from a reasonable distance

Contrary to section 74
Of the road traffic act, 1972. You

Are summoned to appear on 23.5.77
At the hour of 10:00 a.m.

Before the magistrates' Court sitting
At the Court House, Guildhall,

To answer the said
Information and statement of facts.

2
No white light to the front? No red
Light to the rear? O

Constable waters, O pedal cycles
O ancient magistrates and ancient guilds

Of Cambridge: O reason & reasonable distance
O information that's laid

O hours of deepest darkness O lights
Both white & red which flash

Toward the future and signal
The past & the passing: O vision O visions

I was illuminated all over all tingling
Fluorescent & flashing in

Every direction at once: I had read
For a day in your citadels Marlowe O Newton

O John Maynard Keynes
And I've fled to the silts & peats & clays

Of the fens and dug in
And dug into the prehistorical fens

Where I wait for you
With my hoard of knowledge and flints

With my bicycle chain and both of my pedals
With my deer's antler and medals

Where I wait with my middle-American vowels
Where I summon you all

To the Stone-age shaft where I hade & abide
With the ghosts

Of hairy Fenmen: Constable, magistrate, prefect,
Bursar, provost, torturer, cook—

With a bright white light to the front: with
A bright red light to the rear—

I summon you all: all of you: to appear!

Two Poems in Dedication

1. Little Elegy for John Berryman
("Will they set up a tumult in his praise?" *Dream Song* 373)

Oh no, let's not be tumultuous;
Try serene, try gentle
After all. Sane and boring maybe
At the end I hoped
He'd be—Old and hoary like some
Ancient stoic laureate
Who fakes senility in order
To survive—and manages,
And lasts it out.

At the funeral of tenderness
He thought he walked; let's
Have a little then—
Of tenderness, and
Some respect. Because beyond the tumult
And the swagger—deep inside
That house that Henry built—there
Sat down once, serene, a free
And gentle man.

2. Little Apocrypha for Ken Smith

The old Sauk trail, they say,
Still runs under U.S. 12
North from Niles to Detroit.
U.S. 20 takes it west through
Rolling Prairie to Chicago.

You can drive a car that's named
For Cadillac up U.S. 12
To Ypsilanti, turning north
At 94 to a port named for the Hurons.
You can even drive

Your Pontiac to Pontiac.
But only trickster Whiskey's brother
Chibyabos back in
Ken and Eddie's other life
Ever drove in a Tecumseh
To Tecumseh.

Elegy for Clara

I remember milkweed at the shore
and cattail stems which I was
lacing absent-mindedly through oarlocks
of the dingy when I noticed you,
sensual and vulnerable, even
to my inexperienced eyes, a lock of reddish hair
matted at the crotch of your bikini
as you lay there smiling,
sunning on your cousin Cherubini's
new, expensive dock. You looked me over
like you would a flock of hens.
You were The Older Sister of
my new impressive friend, and the setting was
from some bad movie none of us
had seen: the private island and the bathing beach,
the sailboat and the sea.
In the night, your cousin's guests
would all sing barbershop quartets
because your father was insistent that we should
and every moon
must rhyme with June
and like it.
You were a reticent and recent bride
and it was late September.

In the winter, my poor red ears aflame,
infected by the complications
of the February strep, I heard
the gossips saying "Terrible! It's awful"
and I thought at first they meant
the pain I felt. I saw them, bleary, wagging
fingers with my mother by the kitchen sink
where she poured me out
a draught of Nelson's Balsam recommended
by a British shrink we knew.
They said the man who'd married you
demanded you do "awful things"

and so you left him
like you should have—fast—
because one doesn't have to stomach *that*.
I was too terrified and sick
to ask them what they meant, though
I thought I'd die to know it
or else heal.
I stuffed the cotton deeper in my ears
and thought about it off and on
for twenty years.
For twenty years you spent
your life not far from Cherubini's island.

Clara, ageless Older Sister,
I must have thought you were immortal.
Are you really dead at forty-three who wouldn't
have remembered me, my
roving child's eye, the cotton
in my red, infected ears,
who heard the gossips talking and despaired?
Can you accept a stranger's elegy?
I send no flowers
and I do not talk to mourners at your wake
about the things one doesn't have to stomach
or the things that one must take.
I throw no clod of earth onto your grave.
But I am absolutely certain that I loved you once.
And I remember milkweed at the shore
and cattail stems in oarlocks
of the dinghy by the dock
at Cherubini's island in September.

On Lake Michigan
(Sinai, Biafra, Pakistan)

Twenty degrees below the normal for May,
        a heavy mist and fierce wind off the lake:
I cut up logs for the iron pot-bellied stove.
        We came here thinking *enough, enough*
(Of winter & its deaths), and now my daughters
        both are ill, sweating out their fevers
In their sleeping bags...

For days they've complained of the smell:
        Alewives in thousands wash up nightly
On the beach. Early every morning I've buried
        these small, gray fish in piles, clearing
The distance for games... graves everywhere, mounds,
        holding my nose. Doing that, I easily
Forgot those others digging too, though they were not
        nearby... And digging

Not in campgrounds, but in towns; not on private beaches
        but on beach heads; and not to bury alewives
But to bury wives—husbands, daughters, sons—
        under the sand, under the earth with
Them all... Even now, kindling wood to keep
        sick children warm, making awkward
Hands do unfamiliar things a hundred miles from
        a telephone or car, I can easily forget
Enough to think I bring on spring instead of fire.

Back in Columbus, Ohio

Cautiously, hoping that nobody sees,
        I stop my hired car outside your house.
You are not there, but far away
        in California putting your children to bed—
Nor have I seen you once in fifteen years.
        It's past eleven: your mother's floating by
A window in a purple robe, your father's
        reading a book. They have both been sick.
Like all their friends, they've had their
        operations, retired from their jobs, and begun,
To their annoyance, talking—like any poet—
        of the past.

What if we had married? The notion seems
        outrageously absurd, and yet, before our lives
Began in earnest, that, as I recall, was once
        indeed the plan. For years, I preferred your
House to mine, your parents to my own…
        And then I loathed them, thought these shadows
At the window pane were guilty of offenses
        intellectual and moral, that they drove you
Crazy to extremes of anarchy and lust through
        their chaste example & their discipline when
All the virginal austerity was mine.

What I want to do, you see, is to leap from
        the car, pound on the door, and say:
Forgive me! As they stand there staring in the
        Autumn night.… (Perhaps we'd spend
An hour drinking brandy then, and tell long tales,
        and show each other photographs,
And shake hands solemnly at twelve.…) But
        of course I don't do anything like
That at all. I start the car and drive on east
        as far as Philadelphia.

To Vladeta Vučković:
On Our Translation of the Kosovo Fragments

Vladeta the Voyvoda!
                Knight who brings the news
From Kosovo
                to gracious Militsa,
Lazarus's queen,
                sister of the Jugovici,
Daughter of Jug Bogdan—
                that's the stock you're made of!
In the name
                of God Almighty
As they all repeat
                in these old epic poems
We struggle with
                (and even in the name
Of Allah maybe)
                what could ever bring
A hero and a Serb
                to South Bend, Indiana?

Where Ivan Mestrović
                petered out his talent
In the awful portrait busts
                and bland madonnas
Of his exile
                we meet beside
The only decent
                piece of work in town—
His 'Jacob's Well'
                and puzzle over
Fates as dark
                as those of Lazarus
And Milosh Obilich
                sung down centuries
Of Turkish occupation
                by dusty peasant guslers

Who didn't need to know
                that fancy alphabet
Saint Cyril left behind,
                in which reforming Vuk
Spelled out phonetically
                a living language
Where one itches through
                the final syllables of names
And scratches at the surface
                of a destiny
In verbal fragments
                of a people's epic past.

How unlikely, Vladeta,
                that we should meet at all.
In 1941 when I was born
                beside a silly field
Of vegetables
                that noncombatant types
Were urged to cultivate—
                officially they called
Such doubtful husbandry
                a "Victory Garden"—
You at just eighteen
                had taken to the hills
With Tito's partisans
                where every urgent message
Sent to Stalin
                (later on to Churchill)
was the same:
                "More Boots!"
The rugged karst
                that cut away your soles
Kept "the occupier,"
                as the euphemistic
Tour books call him now
                (for after all, he's rich),
An easy target
                in the villages and towns.

Did you swoop right down on him
                like Marko on the Turks?
You did—
                but couldn't live with
Certain knowledge
                of unspeakable reprisals.
Nazi mathematics was
                a good deal easier
To follow than your theory
                of recursive funtions
Hammered out in hiding
                six months later in Vienna—
For every officer
                you blew up in the town
They shot
                a hundred villagers.
And who is more
                within his rights
To moralize on firing squads
                than someone who himself
Would stand before one—
                Trying you summarily, your
Comrades tied you to a tree
                and lined up in a nasty file
With leveled rifles aimed
                to blow your very useful brains
To far less squeamish hills.

You can laugh four decades later
                since you've lived to tell
The tale:
                "But my uncle, who as fate
Would have it, is in charge
                of this grim liquidation,
Couldn't shoot his nephew.
                That was 1941; two years later
And he would have."
                He cut you loose and kicked
You in the ass
                and shouted: *run!*

In the ballad, Vladeta
                survives to tell the queen
What he saw at Kosovo:
                "Tell me knight," she says,
"When you were on
                that wide and level plain
Did you see
                great Lazar riding by?
Did you see my father
                and my noble brothers there?
Did you see the husbands
                of my daughters?"
And Vladeta must tell
                of slaughter and betrayal—
The guslar singing
                mournfully in lines of just
Ten syllables, sliding over
                pauses at the fourth
Where prosodists
                would quickly place
Twin horizontal lines—
                Yes, Vladeta must tell
The queen exactly what
                annihilation feels like.

That I see you sometimes
                standing among memories
Like this other Vladeta
                before the queen
Or Mestrović
                among his early works
Or even like Lord Milosh
                on the open plain
You find, of course,
                unspeakably absurd—
"With my broken
                battle-lance, no doubt,
As all the enemy
                press in upon me fighting
Near the river Sitnitsa.

                    One account says Milosh
Killed twelve thousand
                    Turkish soldiers after
He had polished off
                    The Sultan. In fact they
Took him in the tent and
                    cut off both his arms!"

You open up the slivovitz
                    and go on with your tales
Which, my friend, for all
                    the jokes and ironies
Required for the telling
                    never cease to bleed—
And in your cups you sing
                    to me Prince Lazar's fatal choice,
You sing the ancient
                    downfall of the Serbs.
"*Which Kingdom is it
                    that you long for most?*
That's the question that
                    the falcon asked the Tsar.
If you choose the earth, he said,
                    then saddle horses,
Tighten girths—
                    have your knights put on
Their swords and make
                    a dawn attack against
The Turks: your enemy
                    will be destroyed.
But if you choose the skies
                    then build a church—
O not of stone
                    but out of silk and velvet—
Gather up your forces,
                    take the bread and wine,
For all shall perish,
                    perish utterly,
And you, O Tsar,
                    shall perish with them."

As you break your words
                for our inadequate exchange
And give me phrases which
                in token of their real worth
I give you back in scribbled
                & devalued English notes
I hear you choose the earth
                even as you tell me otherwise
And laughingly declare:
                The skies, the skies!
For you are out there
                on that wide & level plain;
You see yourself
                Great Lazar riding by;
You see the father
                of the Lady's brothers there;
You see the husbands
                of her daughters—
And when your uncle
                cuts you loose
You stumble
                through the villages & hills
Playing tokens
                for survival, whispering
In code to border guards
                & agents, prostitutes & poets,
Fellow travelers and
                their wealthy following
Of contraband tobacconists
                an anagram compounded
Of the talismanic words
                that wound the clocks
In old Ragusa:
                OBLITI PRIVATORUM
PUBLICA CURATE—
                Forget your private business
And concern yourself
                with public life, that's
The gist of it—
                knowing well that only those

A man can trust will whisper
                the correct response.
For if a man's a friend
                he knows that underneath
Those proudly chiseled words
                above the lintel close beside
The Rectors palace
                there's a dusty little shop
Whose owner chalks
                (in lingua franca too!)
Upon a blackboard
                hanging in his narrow window
The reply:
                ANYTIME FRIED FISHES.
And that's the phrase,
                you tell me, answers Latin.
That's the phrase
                that took you underground!

Obliti Privatorum Publica Curate
                you intone, and I cry out:
Anytime Fried Fishes!
                and we hug each other like
Two drunken Slavs
                and weep like sentimental
Irishmen & leave our
                empty bottle on the pedestal
Of Mestrović's well.

Vladeta, my Voyvoda,
                my dear unhappy friend,
There is no Kingdom
                left for us to choose.
Neither of the earth
                nor of the sky.
But peace, peace,
                to all who wander
For whatever reason
                from their stony lands

Bringing all the heavy cargo
              of their legends
Humming in a cipher
              in their lucid, spinning minds!

Three Derivations
from *The Dimensions* of Vladeta Vučković

*

So who descended into the town of my birth
And shook the branch heavy with pearls of frost?

Who rewove the lovely braids of girls' dreams
Into sorrowful willows of widows' woe?
Who invented the first remorse?

I would like to cover his head with the black hood of a monk
So that he neither says yes nor no,
So that he neither says why nor how,
So that he neither talks nor keeps silent,
So that he falls apart
And petrifies in his depravity.

Who was it, then, tempted us all to play tokens?

*

I give you the token so that you neither say black nor white,
Neither it is nor it isn't,
Neither blue nor green, neither I want nor I want not;

I give you the token so that you'll mention neither yellow nor red,
So that you'll neither say that you hear
Nor say that you don't;

So you'll shut up about whether it hurts or it doesn't, or whether
It's easy or hard, or whether
You want it or whether you don't;

I give you the token to maintain the secret of orange
And hide the violet
And hide the bitter and sweet, the cold and the warm,
The all and the nothing.

That you will keep silent I give you the token.

*

So who gives a damn for the Power and the Throne?
Who's hustling whom in the game?
Who's cursing somebody's mother?
Who pours the wine from the wineskin?

This is my shop, this is my business,
I give it only to people I like when I want . . .
And most of the time I don't like, I don't want,
Not today, not tomorrow, not the day after tomorrow.

The dawn is older than the sunset.
The sun is higher than the moon and
Higher than the golden apple on the top of the flagstaff.

Derived and translated in collaboration with the author.

In Praise of Fire

*

It has nobody else
Except for the sun and me

*

It shows itself to the vagrant
It shows itself to the cunning
It shows itself to those in love

Nothing is lost in fire
But only condensed

*

At the edges of the fire
The objects which are not aglow
Or otherwise remarkable
Endure in someone else's time

The bird which alone makes the flock
Flies out of the fire

Take a handful of ash
Or of anything else that is past
And you will see that it is still on fire
Or that it can be fire

*Translated with Vladeta Vučković
from the Serbian of Branko Miljković*

Two Derivations from Branko Milković

1 – Inventory of a Poem

Here before all darkness
Is the darkness which illuminates

After that the freedom of the beast to be a beast
And freedom of the snail to be a snail

Before all else the freedom of the birds to lose their way in space

After that the imagination of love
After that prestige of day over the career of fire

A stone grows heavier if it doesn't change

After that the first employment of useless things
After that the famous cat under the skin of the sphinx

2 – The Past of Fire

It teaches the stars to be scornful
It sleeps in its darkness out of severity

It cohabits with time
Mixing its ash with the freshness of day

It glows: its emptiness glows
Its infirmity enlightens all our roads

The sun is the name of its tyranny
The human heart hides in its betrayals

It acknowledges the north
In old age it blesses the terrible cold

The bird creating itself from its wantonness
Reads the ice from its mind

And the polluted fire in the head, the earlier word
Teaches cruelty to a future dawn

After the Serbian, with Vladeta Vučković

Fifteen Derivations from Branko Miljković

*

Let everyone be left alive with his happiness

*

Observe the lightning high above boredom and hope

*

Between the earth and the fire we choose the fire

*

I greet you incorruptible sunrise of the world

*

I shall hide you in my winter
Eternal spring and frozen dawn
The sun is your enemy
In the name of justice in the name of the desert

The sun revolves the truth changes its place
To those who stay true there remain only lies
But at a truthful place it is cold
At a truthful place nobody raises a home

The frozen bird of fire is the only knowledge
Of the stone that chews its ashes
Of the ashes that negotiate new hope
Of the hope it flies right out of and abandons

The strange dialogue between the fire and bird
Promises a more charming bird and a wiser fire
If they discover a common tongue
The bird and the fire can save the world

*

My heart raises dust over the road
My fall prolongs my life

When the flame expires
It hides in flowers and doesn't feed on a thing
The stars and low-flying birds are its scent
Therefore one might believe all of this

With closed eyes in a tempest that's adored
The birds that start to keen betray the forest
Equilibrium's an affront whose real name is *Sorry*:
A new landscape, suited for retelling.

But a stubborn exaltation of the beast delivers the bird
And along the unconscious path of previous life
The grass goes to paradise with the soul of chamomile
The last flower knocks on the door of the poor

*

When ink ripens to blood everybody will know
That it's the same thing to sing and to die

Wisdom, the stronger one will be the first to relent
Only monsters know what poetry is
Uningratiating thieves of fire
Tied to the mast of a ship that's followed
By underwater songs made hazardous by land
In ripened fruit the conscious sun will know
To substitute the kiss that breathes on all the ash
But no one who comes after us
Will have the strength for courting nightingales
When it's the same thing to sing and to die

*

The earth slowly disappears the mournful earth
Who will bury our hearts and our bones

Where memory doesn't reach a single aim
Neither adding us up nor repeating our days
Tear out my tongue and put in a flower so that
Aimless wandering through a life begins
But no more words but no more words at all
Tomorrow for sure even the cowards will do
What only the brave and righteous can do today
Who in the space between ourselves and the night
Can find a beautiful reason for a different love

*

I want to say your name *Greenmountain*
Green conceived in the womb of the wind
Mountain of heaven and the star of my blood
The corners of the world wrestled for their
Death that in the beginning was spiral & cube
And never found at end the roads we search for them
Over the entire earth they're gone
The profile of their absence guards
The night of the *Greenmountain* and their deaths are
The finest constellation on the south side of heaven
The earth smells of the dead *Greenmountain*
I hear you with the ears of my heart and theirs
No one who died there really is dead
Star of my blood and their *Greenmountain*

*

For those who have drowned

*

In the waters of eternal dream as the sun

*

Died at the bottom of distant landscapes

*

Buried for those whose words

*

Have grown from the earth like remedy and rebellion

*

Let the distant sunflowers bow their heads.

    After the Serbian, with Vladeta Vučković
    (Branko Miljković, from 'Earth and Fire,' 'The Future
    of Fire,' 'To The Earth Right Now,' 'Ballad,' 'To the
    Sea Before I Fall Asleep,' and 'Requiem.')

From a Visit to Dalmatia, 1978

I

Korčula is oleander, cypresses & twisted
fig trees; Korčula is stones—
Lemon trees and stones. Quick mirages
above the stones & olive groves:
Shaky vineyard walls of broken stones and

Stones that must be gathered, piled up
before the shallow roots will
take a tenuous hold
in sandy earth: And shallow stony graves
for Partisan or priest, invader.

Limestone & limestone rock in hills
around Lumbarda, limeface of Sveti Ilija
after Orebič:
        Rockslides and
washed out roads, karst—
a landscape that will break you on its back
or make a sculptor of you —

Lozica, Kršinič, Ivan Jurjevič-Knez.

II

Or if not a sculptor then a fisherman.
Or, it would have once.
        Looking at the empty streets
at noon, Toni Bernidič
tells me it's the woist and hottest
day so far in June—he learned
his English in Brooklyn during the war—
But his house is cool, and so
are the wines: Grk, Pošip, Dingač....
He tells me of the wooden ships

he built, each one taking
him a year: but well made, well made—
The work, he says,
was heavy—pointing to his tools.

Now he has no work: the island's
income is from tourists
and the flushed young men who'd once
have been apprentices
sport their *Atlas* badges, ride their
scooters to the Park or Marco Polo
or the Bon Repos
and show their muscles to the breezy
blue-eyed girls
whose wealthy fathers order loudly
wiener schnitzel

wienerschnitzel and stones.

Two Poems

1 – THE EGYPTIAN

Where you descend, depth exists no more.
It was enough that I took your breath away in a reed
For a seed to burst in the desert under my heel.

It all came at a single blow, and nothing remains.
Nothing but the mark on my door
Made by the embalmer's burning hands.

2 – THE URN

Endlessly to watch a second night come on
While looking through this sluggish lucid pyre
Which doesn't even yield any ash!

But the mouth at the end, the mouth that's full
Of earth and rage,
Remembers that it is itself which burns

And guides the cradles on the river.

From the French of Jacques Dupin

Fragments after Hamsun

1

And you who sit up
In the darkness of your cell
And see a glowing word
Before your eyes: KUBOAA.

Who's to tell you that
Your word must signify *tobacco shop*?
Who will say KUBOAA
Must mean *cattle show* or *queen*?

Who's insisting on *heraldic bird*
Or *sunrise*? Who will threaten
You with words like *bread* and *key*?

2

The man who hungers now, who thirsts,
Is made of words like *abattoir*
Himself, although he thinks he's made
Of *sunrise*, *bread* and *key*.

KUBOAA seeks Amanuensis for
His creature with a pen
Whose lips still murmur FÜHRER
North of Bergen!

Free Translation and Recombination: Fragments from Octavio Paz

No vi girar las formas hasta desvanecerse
En claridad inmóvil...

*

By negation is my increase, my wealth.
Lord, Lord of erosions and dispersions,
I come to you in the whirlwind.

Into the oldest tree I drive my nail.

*

In the architecture of silence
Is no debate between the bees
And the stastics.

Nor is there any dialectic among apes.

The wind blows. The rain obliterates
The mason's mark. On every psalm (on every
Mask of lime) a crown of fire appears.

*

To rattle semantic seeds:
To bury the word, the kernel of fire,
In the body of Ceres:

    poem, poem

Spilling the water and wine,
Spilling the fire.

*

Shake the book like a branch,
Detaching a phrase:

Voices and laughter,
Dancing and tambourines.

This is the winter solstice,
Who will awaken the stones?

Shake the book, detaching a word:
Pollywog, poison, periwig…

Say it: a penance of words.

*

But the huddled men in the alleys,
The huddled men in the squares & the mosques,
They took my gems and my grave-clothes.

      I was covered with poems.

In the center of incandescence,
In the column of noon,
I was ringed with sand and insomnia.

      I was covered with poems.

*

And the sophistry of clocks.
And the provinces of abstract towns.

Dizzy geometries, vertigoes.

Not to foretell but to tell.
To say it: a paring away.

Nombre Antiguo del Fuego

    In the tunnels of onyx
            the circles of salt
    Chimerical child of
            calculus and of thirst:

From every stone appears a brief black tongue
Naming the scales of the night.

A Wind in Roussillon

I

The Tramontane that's blowing pages
of an unbound book through Roussillon
departs on schedules
of its own....

Et nous, les os... et nous, les os.
And us, the bones.

II

The train departs from Austerlitz on time.
After Carcassonne, Tuchan,
wheat and barley dry up in the sun
& trees appear hung heavily
with cherries, lemons, oranges.

Red tiled roofs are angled oddly
on the little houses in the hills below Cerdagne.
Gray slate's left behind.

By the tracks
a villager has nailed up a goat's foot
and a sunflower to the door
that opens on his vineyard
circled by a wall of heavy stones.

III

In French, the words of Mme T. about les îles Malouines sound nearly as bizarre as ads for the religious kitsch at Lourdes translated into English in the same edition of *Le Monde*… "A see-through plastic model of the Virgin with unscrewable gold crown enables you to fill the image up with holy water from a tap." And Mme T, *qui a felicitée les forces armées*, swells in French to the dimensions of a Bonaparte: *le plus merveilleuses du monde… le courage et l'habileté ont donné une nouvelle fierté à ce pays et nous ont fait comprendre que nous étions vraiment une seule famille.*

Et nous, les os: vraiment une seule famille.

IV

Low hills dense with yellow broom!
Cactus, thistles, wild mountain roses;
lavender and holly and convolvulus.
Above the rows of plane trees,
olive groves root down through rock.
Above the olive groves, cypresses & pines.

Down the valley under Canigou
a helicopter dips and passes overhead,
circles the Clinique Saint-Pierre
whining like a homing wasp.
Landing in an asphalt parking lot,
it scatters old men playing skittles, boules.
Young men wearing orange flight suits
carry something human
wrapped in white inside.

V

The name of one low, ruined house
in Perpignan is John
and Jeanne. (It's in another country.)
When great winds pass the threshold
nothing sings or appears.

It's John & Jeanne
and from their graying faces
falls the plaster of day. (Far off
the most ancient one,
the arch daughter of shadows.)

You build a fire in the cold great hall
and you withdraw.
(Your name is Yves Bonnefoy.)
You build it there, and you withdraw.

VI

My hostess came to Perpignan from Dublin more than forty years ago. Now in her late sixties, she lives in the third floor flat of an elegant eighteenth-century house in what were once the servants' quarters. The walls are full of books on Cathar heresies and Albigensians and Templars. When the south of France was flayed for twenty years in the Crusades, blood ran all the way from Montségur to the Quéribus Château before it finally dried. Mme Danjou came here with the Quakers when the Spanish Civil War broke out and helped Republican refugees across the border at Port Bou. Four years later she was helping Jews across the border in the opposite direction when the Roussillon was occupied by the Nazis. Denounced by a neighbor, she was thrown in jail where she waited for the train that would take her to a prison camp in Germany. Like other European women of her generation, she is tough. "One felt," she says, struggling for a moment with the English that she rarely speaks these days, "that one had work to do." The war had ended by the time the Nazis sent the train.

VII

Not only the delimited circumferences
but also all the white stone houses
in the streets of southern Catholic cemeteries
speak of walled towns by Vauban
or by his foretypes in the Middle Ages or before.
This silent town within the town of Collioure
where Derain and Picasso paid their bills
with paintings no one wanted yet
fortifies itself against the naked bathers
and the tourists at the Templiers.
I intrude upon the silent tenants searching
for Antonio Machado.

The wealthy dead inhabit their expensive homes
and wait impatiently for quick descendants
to arrive and fill each empty room marked reservée.
The poor lie down in dresser drawers stacked high
in marble walls around a central Calvary
and whisper without any *nouvelle fierté a ce pays:*
"Nous étions vraiment une seule famille."

Machado fled from Franco's armies
first to Barcelona, then across the border
with some refugees. Dying, he came
on foot, and in the rain, and with his mother.
He left the room they gave him only once
to walk alone along the streets of Collioure
before they brought him here.
He sings these dead his mortal words forever.
Globo del fuego… disco morado…

The sun that parched the bones
dries up the town, dries up the southern sea.
Savilla is distant and alone.
Sol. Soleil.
Castile, and Collioure! Machado.

VIII

With knife or nail or glass someone clumsily
has scratched into the blackened wooden gate
that's chained high up beyond one's reach
at Fort Saint-Elme: *Privée, Bien Gardée.*

A small green lizard darts between two stones.
It looks to be deserted in the tower, and yet
it's difficult to tell. Everything inside
has been restored. They say it's lived in now.

Climbing here, I heard two cuckoos answering
each other down the valley. A kestrel hovers high
and drops to earth the far side of the tower.
No sound now but northern wind on fortified étoile.

The level sea below me mirrors Le Château Royal
that Dugommier won back for revolution after
Dufour's treason turned the cannon of Saint-Elme
on quiet Collioure for money and for Spain.

From the col de Banyuls through Port-Vendres
they'd advanced. Then, bien gardee, Saint-Elme.
A captain stood about where I stand, bargaining.
Dufour let him quickly through the gates.

No one sang the cruel cannonade they loosed
on the Château which burned away the Middle Age
from rampart, hall and tower. Dugommier won back
the smoking bones before which once some

pitiful last troubadour sang out to Templars
gazing down at him beside the sea. No one gazes
down from Fort Saint-Elme. Nor do I sing out
Dòna, Maries de caritat...

                                  Lady, mother of charity...
I was born too late....

IX

Tour de la Massane, Tour de Madeloc. Towers like these stretch along the backbone of the Pyrenees and look down on the plain of Roussillon, the southern coast, and Spain. By day the little garrisons would signal to each other with a puff of smoke, by night with fire. Valerius Flaccus, Commandant at Madeloc, left his chiselled mark on the great rock. In Rome, they put him on a coin. In Roussillon, *les os. Que malvaise chanson de nos chanté ne seit*, he might have said a little later and little to the west. What he said, in fact, was this:

> VALERIUS FLACCUS
> PRAEFECTUS PRAESIDII MONUMENTUM JUSSIT
> VIVUS SIBI CONDI LOCO
> INTERCEPTO ET EMUNITO

The buried temple spits no mud or rubies out. The sun pours down upon the tower that now relays the television news from Paris, London, Rome, and even as far off as Lebanon or Las Malvinas. I sit in my hotel and drink in martial music from the streets of Buenos Aires. Then we see Israeli tanks annihilate Beirut. Communication is a subtle thing through our electric sepulchre. In the Punic wars, Valerius could only talk in hyperbolic terms with smoke and fire.... Power hymns instalments to its spirit now in all works of impatience: wars, towers, rituals, TV. In memory, Valerius, you arise. Like an occult language found in an iron-bound book

X

Mother of charity, Mother of consolation,
Your house is not La Tour Madeloc,
Mother of bones, Mother of dissolution.

Lady of leisure, Lady of Roussillon,
Maître Xinxet has blackened your hermitage,
Lady of landfall, Lady of languors.

Mother of ostentation, Mother of ordure,
Neptune rests in your chapel,
Mother of noon, Mother of nightshade.

Lady of purdah, Lady of purchase,
The village cries out for rain,
Lady of drought, Lady of departures.

Mother of Jesus, Mother of jackals,
The pilgrim is flaying the Jew,
Mother of olives, Mother of obeisance,

Lady binding the book in leather & iron,
Mother of scattered pages,
Work of secret patience, Tramontane.

Part V

Four Monologues
and a Song Cycle Text

Findings from 1973-1993

The Old Master's Plaine Style Complainte

Ardent fight stayeth a gardant fight
    or putteth back
    or beateth
Open fight stayeth an open fight
Variable answereth variable
Close fight is beaten by gardant fight

Slowfoot: swift hand   Quickfoot: slow hand

    tread, stride, follow, fallaway

    ...they seek a true defense in an untrue sword
Rapiers! Frogpricking poniards! The strange devices of
Italians and the French. Toys fit to murer poultrie, I
Should say. My Lord:
              THEY BRING THEIR LIVES
    TO AN END BY ART

        Can they pierce a corslet
            or unlade a helmet strap?
        Can they hew asunder pikes?

Tempestuous terms

    streta, dritta, reversa

Our best men fall to style.

Speak not evil? Behind the backs of Men? Dispraise no play
Nor workmanship? But Italians! We answer the bragging
Strangers, we point: Signoir Rocko and Signoir Rocko his son

        with false play or plaine
        with broken shins, cracktpates.

...for Rocko came to town, all right, and built himself a fancy place in Warwick Lane. Not a fencing-school, mind you, but a *college*. Styled himself the World's Greatest Master Of The Art. (And teaching *offense!*) His scholars—noblemen and gentlemen of the court—would set up their arms: and under these their gear: rapiers and daggers, gloves of mail and gauntlets.... He was the darling of the sycophants and courtiers: much beloved by men who never need to draw a sword, men of elegance and wit, men of leisure, poets: men who can afford a fashion or a style. One day Austen Bagger, being merrie and amongst his friends, took his sword and buckler and his valiant heart off to Warwick Lane, and standing there upon his skill he shouted: ROCKO, YOU FAGGOT, UP YOUR ASS WITH BOATMEN'S OARS AND BATTLE AXE AND PIKE. UP YOUR ASS WITH RAPIERS...

> And down came Rocko with his two hand sword
> > And manfully did Austen Bagger close with him
> And stroke up his heels
> > And cut him under the breech...

> Shall I admonish against quarrels and brawls?
> I tell you: Judgment, Distance; Time & Place and Measure
> I do not darkly ryddle here
> I set it down

> I choose, my Lord,
> The short and ancient weapons of our land.

The times are difficult, and have been. I tell you plainly that our Masters of Defense are thought by those who flatter Bobadill to be so many vagabonds and bearwards. The city fathrs, fearing, as they say the plague, will have no prizes played in London. But any haberdasher sells to any cobbler bucklers. Every serving man will play with hilted cudgels squaking in the language of Italian schools. But Richard Beste? Gunner at the Tower. William Hearne? Yeoman of the guard. William Joyner? Tavern keeper. John Evans? Jerkin-maker Honest men and masters of a mystery, but all of them pretending trades beause the law from Coke and Blackstone on has always here and still will threaten penalties...

> I mean the Statute of Rogues
> I mean the Vagrancy Act
> I mean to say I'm not among the lewd and dissolute who'd
> > covet singular advantage without license or authority or oath

> I'd teach a man to fight!

So here's
Our bargain Sir
And guild or no incor-
Poration patent royal favour
Ipso facto lawful sworn I swear it
On a hilt which is to say the cross KNOW
YE THAT WE admit all provosts of sufficient
Cunning expert tried before us masters of the science
Openly within the city giving scholars first a warning twenty
Days and then to playe their prize by god or sovereign lady queen
Of England France and Ireland all her sherifbaylif's deputies and con-
Stables we certify commission and we license deputise
Defenders of the realm of England
By the grace of god

      amen

The weapons are not rapiers. The weapons are the longsword sword and buckler backsword sword and dagger stave or pike the great two-handed sword the single dagger javelin the partisan the black bill glaive and half-pike battle axe . . .

    . . . and these are times:

        The time of the hand
           The time of the hand and bodie
           The time of the hand, body and foot

      The time of the foot
         The time of the foot and bodie
         The time of the foot, bodie and hand

. . . this is not mathematics this is movement. This is not manners: This is not ballet. Whatsoever is done with the hand before the foot or feet is true. Whatsoever is done with the foot or feet before the hand is false. I tell you: Judgment, Distance; Time & Place & Mesure. I tell you grips and wrestlings. I tell you thrusts and blows. Treading of ground, doubles, wards, closing and breaking, knees to the groin, boot in the ass, knife in the eyes: There is not observation of Italian niceties in War.

And now there are more of them.
I mean Saviolo and Co.

Business is bad…

...out poets advertise their doings on the stage and yet not one of them will play his prize. They stay indoors and write their books and talk of etiquette. They read Castiglione, draw their diagrams from Euclid, darn their hose, inspire all diversities of lies. All of them are pedarasts. They dance the galliard and pavane, they vault most nimbly, oh they caper loftily these warlike souls who translate greek and perish from the French disease…

Hieronimo, go by. Well *he* got *his* at least.

They'll touch the weapons of another man that weareth them yet deal with all punctilio to be observed. They talk of noble ancestors in Rome.

> They boast outrageously
> > They dye their beards
>
> They only feign
> > They will not fight

These euphuistic lurid sodomites…

TAKE UP FENCING! Drive away all aches and pains; drive away disease and grief, make a nimble body, get thee strength. It sharpeneth the wit, expelleth choler, melancholy, many other vile conceits: it keepeth man in breath, in perfect health, it makes him to be long of life who useth it … Item, item, item! You shall swear so help you god that you shall uphold and maintain such articles as shall be here delivered unto you … Item, item, item! Loving truth and hating falsehood you shall be a master to the last day of your life. Item, item, item! You shall not any suspect person teach, no murderer nor common quarreler no drunkard no nor shall you mix with them…

> You shall be merciful.
> You shall love and honor him who taught you cunning.
> Item, item, item…

useless!

I weep for Master Turner: murdered with a pistol from behind.
I weep for Henry Aldington: hanged.
I weep for Furlong: drunk a pint of aqua vita straight off
    in one go; then he fell down dead.
I weep for Westcott: suicide.

    …for there are wicked angels which are waiters
and attend upon ungodly life … attend upon

        the time of the hand
            the time of the hand and bodie
        the time of the hand, bodie and foot

    …and then he need not fear to say *Come Quickly*: today or tomorrow or when thou wilt, and with what manner of death soever, so it come by thine appointment

    I think I'll go get Saviolo myself.
    I'll challenge him, call him out of his
    Elegant house, away from his elegant friends.

    I'll close with him. I'll strike up his heels.
    I'll cut him under the breech.
    I'll take his salp. I'll take his scalp.

    I'll vanish quick (quick!) to Illyria.

A Cambridge Spinning-House
Henry John Temple Palmerston's Syllabics
For Marianne Moore

I too dislike it
    but the matron shall have
no occupation or calling but that
    of matron
of the house She shall reside
    on the premises
and not
    be absent for a night without permission

I too dislike it
    but she shall cause a print
ed copy of the rules respecting the
    inmates to
be hung up in every cell
    and shall read or cause
to be
    read the said rules to every inmate upon

her committal I
    too dislike it She shall
learn these rules herself and observe them well
    and as far
as possible cause them to
    be observed by all
I too
    dislike it but she must enter in her book

everything that she
    sees and hears She shall rule
her roost and exercise her authori
    ty with firm
ness temper and humani
    ty and abstain from
language
    and remarks that might be seen as calcula

ted to irritate
    an inmate She shall at
tend to the employments and industri
    al training
of inmates follow the di
    rections of the chap
lain with
    regard to their instruction and assist by

her influence and
    authority his ex
ertions for the reformation I too
    dislike it
The cells she must visit and
    frequently inspect
also the
    yard kitchen and other parts of the house She

shall occasional
    ly go through the house at
an uncertain hour of the night and re
    cord in her
journal the hour of the vis
    it and the state of
the house
    at the time She shall see the inmates locked up

at night in their cells
    at eight o'clock and shall
have the gate of the house locked and the key
    placed in safe
keeping She shall enforce a
    high degree of clean
liness
    in every part of the house and also in

the person of the
    inmates their clothing bed
ding and everything in use She shall take
    every pre

caution against the escape
        of an inmate and
she shall
        examine the windows doors bars bolts and locks

I too dislike it
        but the inmates shall keep
their cells and the furniture and uten
        sils therein
clean and in good order They
        shall be clean and neat
in their
        persons wash their hands and faces daily and

wash their feet or bathe
        at least once a week or
as often as the matron shall direct
        no inmate
shall disobey the orders
        of the matron or
other
        officers of the house or treat with disre

spect any of the
        officers or servants
or any person visiting the house
        or employed
therein or be idle or
        negligent in her
work or
        willfully damage the same or absent her

self without leave from
        divine service or the
daily prayers or behave irreverent
        ly thereat
or be gulty of any
        indecent or im
moral
        language or conduct or use any provok

ing or abusive
    words or converse or hold
intercourse with any other inmate
    in a way
not authorized by the rules
    of the house or cause
annoy
    ance or disturbance by singing or making

a noise or pass or
    attempt to pass out of
her cell or beyond the bounds of the room
    or place where
she may be employed or dis
    figure the walls or
other
    parts of the house or deface secrete destroy

or pull down any
    paper or notice hung
up by authority in or about
    the house or
willfully injure any
    clothing bedding or
other
    article or commit any nuisance or

have in her cell or
    possession any ar
ticle not furnished by the establish
    ment or give
or lend to or borrow from
    any other in
mate an
    y food book or other article without

leave or refuse or
    neglect to conform to
the rules regulations and orders of
    the house The

matron may examine an
    y inmate touching
such of
    fences and determine thereupon and may

cause any inmate
    so offending to be
punished by being closely or other
    wise confined
in a dark or light cell or
    dislike it dislike
it I
    too dislike it I too dislike

I certify the foregoing Rules as proper
to be enforced in the Spinning-House at Cambridge

Whitehall, 21 Feb. 1854. PALMERSTON.

Mr. Rothenstein's Rudiments

It's strange. I told that pretty girl yesterday
that, yes, I knew her mother, but I knew her
great-grandmother too – Lady Burne-Jones.
It's even stranger, thinking on it, that I met
Rossetti's brother as a child; I can see
him clearly lying on that couch I rescued
for the Tate—the one on which the poet's friends
placed Shelley's body when they took it from the sea—
when I heard the house, Rossetti's, took a hit
during the blitz.   My father knew them all, of course—
Sir William! Whistler and Degas, Rodin, Pater,
Swinburne, Henry James. After the Slade he went
to Paris and he might have stayed,
except that Basil Blackwood, then at Balliol,
commissioned him to make that portrait drawing
that initiated the entire Oxford series
published by John Lane. So home he came and
grew more earnest reading Tolstoy, speaking
much of probity. A French Benedictine,
and later also Eric Gill, thought
he should enter an order, or anyway go paint
at Ditchling Common. He stayed in London, though,
and met Augustus John and all the younger men.
As the influence of Whistler waned, his line began
to grow a little thick, his canvasses
just a little cluttered.

Augustus John. And Gwen. Do you realize
we nearly had Gwen John in bronze on the embankment?
Every time I stand before the *Burghers of Calais*
I see poor Gwen. She posed for Rodin when he did
the plaster for a Whistler monument, holding
a medallion of her teacher. But because it lacked an arm—
I'd guess that half his figures lack an arm or leg—
the jury opted for a casting of the *Burghers* and
Augustus found his sister, after she had died, leaning

back against a wall in some obscure dark corner
of a Paris shed. I mean of course he found
the plaster of his sister…

    …Anyone who'd say that Stanley Spencer
is inferior to Arp or Mondrian can't see!
Everybody followed Fry and then got stuck somehow
on all those formal theories and by what
you'd have to call an orthodoxy after being bowled away
by Post-Impressionism. Give me Stanley Spencer
to a watered-down Matisse by Duncan Grant.
Besides, his charater's of interest.
And the more we know about him and the world
he inhabited the more we see in what he made.
I'd say that's true of any artist. Also we can sometimes
understand the way a man can fill his art with
all the qualities and virtues that his life most lacks—
And that's a knowledge I prefer to Mr. Fry's
aesthetics and all the revolutions of a Herbert Read.

Stanley! He came one night to dinner, missed
his train to Cookham, and then stayed on
for something like three months. He'd talk all day,
all night: Cookham and his painting.
His father read the bible to his children every night
and every morning Stanley walked through Cookham
seeing all the stories re-enacted in his village
by the Thames. In a way, he really did believe
they had occurred there—Jerusalem,
the emanation of his Cookham youth!
Look at his *Nativity*, his *Zacharias* and *Elizabeth*.
When I acquired the *Resurrection* for the Tate,
half of London sneered, half the critics
simply thought him crazy. Then they condescended,
calling him "a village pre-Raphaelite"—Spencer,
whose *Zacharias* I'd be willing to compare
even with Giotto…
    He did travel a bit after the war—
as far as China once. When Chou En-Lai remarked
he hoped these English now would know New China,

Stanley said he hoped New China might one day
Know Cookham....

      Wyndham Lewis
Didn't come from Cookham—
much more likely Mars. He arrived in London
like some trigger-happy extraterritorial
and took on everything and everyone in sight.
I knew him pretty well. And yet he'd be so
secretive he wouldn't even let you know he had
a wife after he'd been married several years.
She'd make the dinner for her husband and a guest,
set the table, then just disappear...

Of course it was the Fry affair, the mess
at Omega, that was much responsible
for Lewis's mistreatment by the crowd
that wanted to control a nation's taste.
He claimed that Fry had stolen his commission
To design a sitting-room for the *Daily Mail's*
model home exhibit, then in compensation offered
him an overmantel whre he'd be allowed
to execute a carving. So Lewis sent that letter
to the press about *a timid but voracious
journalistic monster* that finished him with
Bloomsbury and Fry. But in an age of log-rolling,
as he said himself, Mr. Lewis
never once was rolled...

      Do you realize
that no one ever had convincingly portrayed
an ordinary business suit before the Lewis *Eliot*?
I mean with full verisimilitude, without
somehow ennobling it. There sits the poet—
in the suit he'd worn at Lloyds!

The editor of *Blast* and friend of Ezra Pound
went to war in the artillery, then came home
and painted *Bagdad, Barcelona, Stations of the Dead*.
He said his geometrics wanted filling

and he filled them with inventions, not
with the matter of the continental Cubists.
I heard him say of Braque that one might very well
be musical or vegetarian, but life was more
than mandolins and apples.

      And more (or maybe less!)
than all those decorations on the walls
at Charleston as well, that strange domestic
Sistine Chapel down in Sussex. I thought I'd better
go there and make my peace with Mrs. Bell
when I decided I should write on Duncan Grant.
It was not a happy visit.
I guess I said that it was my opinion
Titian couldn't draw. Anyway, she glared at me
as if I'd shot the gun that killed her son in Spain.
I've tried to do an honest job on Grant—
mainly as a decorator and the artist
of the Holland portrait and the two of Mrs. Bell.
Still, it's difficult to make ambitious claims for him
like those put forward by his friends—

and also difficult, sitting there at Charleston,
the light pouring on a garden full of flowers and
through a window on the decorated walls, the pottery,
the accumulations of a privileged life, not to think
about a painter like Gwen John, isolated and unknown,
or of my father as his reputation steadily declined
and he sat alone on the terrace at Far Oakbridge
gazing at the contours of the valley in his illness,
looking through the beauty of this world
at something he could almost see behind it.

   (Cento: Passages & paraphrase from John Rothenstein's
    Modern English Panters. Variation, derivation,
       & apocrypha)

Auto Icon

My body I give

        to my dear friend
        Doctor Southwood Smith

        to be disposed of

in manner herinafter mentioned

And I direct that…
he will take my body under his charge
and take the requisite and appropriate measures

        for the disposal
        and preservation

of the several parts of my bodily frame

in the manner expressed in the paper
annexed to this my will
and at the top of which I have written

        AUTO ICON

The skeleton he will cause to be put together
in such manner as that the whole figure
may be seated in a chair
        usually occupied by me
when living
in the attitude in which I am sitting
when engaged in thoughts
in the course of the time
employed in writing…

I direct that the **BODY** thus prepared
shall be transferred by my executor

He will cause the skeleton to be clad
in one of the suits of *black*
>					occasionally
>					worn
>					by me.

The **Body** so clothed (together with the chair
and the staff in my later years
born by me)

he will take charge of

>			**AND**
>			for containing the whole apparatus
>			he will cause to be prepared

an appropriate **BOX** or **CASE**
and he will cause to be engraved

>			*in conspicuous characters*

on a plate to be affixed thereon
(and also on the labels on the glass cases
in which the preparation
of the Soft Parts of my Body
shall be contained)

>			**My Name**
>			at length

>			with the letters
>			**O.B.**

>			followed by the date of my decease.

If it should so happen
that my personal friends
>			(and other disciples)
should be disposed to meet together
on some day or days of the year

for the purpose of commemorating
the founder of the

Greatest Happiness System

of morals and legislation
my executor will (from time to time)
cause to be conveyed

> to the room in which they meet
> the said BOX or CASE

with the contents
there to be stationed in such part of the room
as to the assembled company

shall seem

> meet.

> (Found in the will of Jeremy Bentham and first
> commissioned as poem from John Daniels: JM,
> ed. *23 Modern British Poets*, 1970)

Song Cycle Awaiting a Setting
Tenor, Baritone, Soprano

I — AFTER HEINE
Tenor

The night is still, sleeping in the streets,
And still the house in which my lover lived.
She is sleeping somewhere else and yet
Her house in this same place stands still.
Time stands still. Still as well the man who stands
And stares into her window—someone else,
But also me. In the moonlight, me—
But also someone else: Doppelgänger
Made of me and wringing hands, who shakes
With grief and rage, dark and doublegoer,
Pale companion, *mon semblable, frère,*
Who makes my *Liebesleid* his own, takes
The night that's mine, takes in stillness now
My lover and my witness and my love.

II – AFTER GEORGE SEFERIS

1 — Euripides the Poet
Baritone

Euripides the poet
Growing old between the holocaust at Troy
And the Reichstag fire
Beheld the sea and heard the oceanic laughter
Of the gods. He liked the sea-shore caves
Where he could be alone
And try to see the net of human veins, designed
To capture us like animals, as something
To be torn and broken through.
He was a bitter, friendless man. When he died,
He died not in Athens but in Macedon
Where dogs ate his flesh and dragged his bones
Around and around the city walls.

2 — Isaac and Iphigenia
Tenor

And Isaac said: This is my body, my flesh.
To Iphigenia, whose father was not
Halted in his work by any intervening hand,
I offer it in marriage, though I am but a boy
And she a virgin bleeding from her throat.
She will take me to her, she will fondle me. I will
Be entirely hers. Our fathers should have met.
Imagine Agamemnon saying "Abraham!"
And Abraham responding "Agamemnon!" Imagine
Poets asking them: Who is to be saved,
Who is to be sacrificed? Our dear son will know.
Our dear daughter will reveal it. But first we will praise
The Many and the One, the Lord
And the lords, the Father and our fathers,
And all the calculating gods and God.

2 — Iphigenia and Isaac
Soprano (Alternative: Spoken, *sotto voce*, on electronic tape)

And Iphigenia said: This is not my body, my flesh.
From Isaac, whose father was interrupted
In his work by an intervening hand, I withhold *I am*.
They told me I had come to an altar for Achilles
And I found another child like me. I wept to behold him.
Agamemnon never held out hands to Abraham.
Our fathers never met. No one knows or will know who
Is led to sacrifice and who is saved before the hour.
I was the hour. Only we are daughter and the son.
I think we are spirits lingering beyond our time, for
They have truly murdered me. Troy and The Temple fell.
Let poets curse the many and the One, the Lord
And the lords, the Father and our fathers,
And all the calculating gods, and God.

III – After Gunnar Ekelöf: *Xoanon*
For Baritone and Tenor

Tenor:
I possess, in you, a wonder-working Icon
If possessing something is to possess nothing
As she possesses me. Thus I possess her.
She was given me on the very day she 'appeared'
At a pre-ordained time, at an appointed place
And the same *Panayía* is revealed again
Whenever the heart so desires. Leaning on her arm
Stands, in ceremonial robes, on an inversely
Perspectival stool, a grown-up infant in arms
Who is the last prince of my line.
I lift him away, for every attribute
Belonging to this *Panayía* can be lifted away
As a plunderer dislodges a silver smith's *basmá*
From a picture kissed so much
The hands have darkened and fallen apart.

Baritone
I lift the crown and the two criers of joy
From their cloud and golden ground in the upper corners.
I disengage the ornamental clasp from the *Maphorion*
And lift the veil from her hair and from her neck.
I free the folds across her right breast
And carefully the folds across her left
Aching with pain. I lift like a spider's web
The thin undergarment, which leaves the enigma
At once resolved and unresolved, and she looks at me
With brown irises in the blue white of her eyes—
Keeps looking at me…

Baritone and Tenor

      We disengage her arms
Her brown hand with its rose, the brown breasts—
The right one first, the left one carefully last,
Aching with pain—and then the girdle after kissing it.
We lift her forehead, her hairline and her cheeks

And finally her big eyes which look at us,
Keep looking at us, even after they are taken away.
We lift the golden ground and the priming
Until the wood with its thick graining is bared:
A bit of an old olive plank, sawed off
A tree felled by a storm, in a time long ago
On some northern coast. There, in the tree,
Almost overgrown, appears the eye of a sprig
Broken off when the tree was still young—
You keep looking at us. *Hodigítria, Philoúsa*

Xoanon: version co-translated with Lars-Håkan Svensson

Part VI

Early Poems (2)

For Michael Anania and Peter Michelson
First readers of these poems

I Gather the Bones of *Bucyrus*

"Let the poet who has been not too long ago born make very sure of this, that no one cares to hear that he feels sprightly in spring, is uncomfortable when his sexual desires are ungratified, and that he has read about human brotherhood in last year's magazines."
         Ezra Pound, *I Gather The Limbs of Osiris*

To the sprightly in spring

To the gratification of desire

To the human brotherhood in last year's magazines

Two Graffiti

I – An Essay on Aesthetics

The fetishism of the displaced craftsman,
The craft of the misplaced fetishist:
O gather me into the orifice of eternity.

II – Take That!

Because my wife is beautiful
There are occasions in my life
For old prohibited emotions
Such as jealousy and lust.

Thus my heart goes out
To the man who, craning his neck
For a better look at her,
Missed the unmarked turn
And wrecked his car.

Smoking Cigars with a Friend in Northern Indiana

"Call the roller of big cigars..." —Wallace Stevens

My friend Ed Goerner smokes cigars and
tells me why he smokes cigars:

His *father* smoked cigars, because
his father made cigars, the union kind,

that's why. He offers me a fat black
brute with brandy after dinner, peels the

label off his own, snips the end, lights up,
leans back, and blows the heavy smoke

with satisfaction into early spring night air.
I light up too, and listen, sitting on

a porch in South Bend, Indiana.
My granddad, Goerner says, *arrived in*

New York fresh from Denmark as a kid
of say sixteen: he had a letter with him

written to a person with a name eight
hundred other people answered to

in New York City: just the name & no address.
Some Germans working in tobacco took him in

after he had nearly starved wandering
the streets and looking for the one among

eight hundred in the phone book with that name
who might have known his uncle once.

*He never found him but he learned his German
and he learned to roll cigars—in a union shop*

*of course where they screened you for TB.
(If you smoked cigars without the label it was*

*risky: all those sick non-union types would
lick the final leaf to stick it down & then*

*you'd have it too: TB.) They had a full-time
job called "Reader" in those heady days*

*who'd read aloud from Goethe or from Heine
all day long while all those rollers rolled.*

*The union then was keen on self-improvement.
My granddad knew a thousand lines by Heine*

*and could play ten parts from 'Faust,' and all
of this from memory: he never read a book.*

*When the reader gave up poetry for Marx, all
those union rollers listened, start to finish,*

*to 'Das Kapital.' In the end my granddad
was converted as he rolled and rolled and rolled*

*and statistics routed poetry for good. When
the reader finished Marx he started out on Engels.*

Goerner asks for my cigar, tears off
the label I had left in place, quotes a line

from Lenin, puts the label in his mouth,
and swallows it: *And that*, he says,

*is why I smoke cigars and why my father
smoked cigars: they're incense for the roller's*

bread and wine of Socialist Communion!

Diptych

1

Carpet flames.
Chain grip: incense
in a cup. Violins
and mandolins re-
corded. Oddly off.
Stumble dancer,
rafter slanting down.
(What is now beyond
you now and dear?)
Hold it (having
hardened) with a kiss.
He had lied
for years.

          2

          Zero on ice.
          Tire spun: smoke
          to three a.m. Hail
          and also headlight
          dimming. Oddly out.
          Weep then weeper,
          headlight out and hail.
          (Who is now beside
          me now and dear?)
          Break it (having
          buckled) with a fist.
          She had cried
          for years.

Five Alchemical Lyrics

1.

Sing-bonga, angered
by the smoke, sent
crows. Later he slept
in the furnace.

Sing-anga, earlier
and far away, a
fetus found and
burned:
> *On that ash*
> *erect a temple, Yakut shaman.*

Yang & Yin
Yin & Yang

For the smith
and his bride,
these coals.

2.

Could boil, melt
(ego in hand)
his world

Therefore feared
as agent
("public menace")

Matter unregenerate
mirrors (crime)

Verbum dictum factum: God in
the vowels of the earth:

Ascribe unto
these metals, Hermes,
need

3.

(otherwise
perceive the imperfection
understand

not to imperfection
even otherwise
command

dross & refuse &
decay

ascend
condense)

Philosophy, he held, was out of hand.

4.

Whether C. was
       Duped *per doctrinam*
Whether C. knew
       Shuchirch at all

William de Brumley, "chaplain lately
dwelling with the Prior of Harmondsworth"—
does he lie?

Whether C. was
a victim or student…

       (hermaphroditic rebis
       there appeared)

Probably not)

Probably not

later,
after

5

The still-providing
world is not
enough: we add

ponder matter
where impatient
sleepers wait.

And Aphrodite
saw her soul
was stone.

And Nargajuna
dreamed that
he was glad.

Herman's Poems

1

We suffer
and we're there, all right?
Baby, douse the light.

(Herman's hawking
severed heads
and hands.)

We suffer
and we're there, all right?
Not this time of night.

(Herman's hawking
severed heads
and hands.)

Herman is in
bed with us.
Herman's on the tree.

(Herman's hawking
severed heads
and hands.)

We suffer
and we're there, all right?
Baby, douse the light.

Herman doesn't care
for you and me.

2

People's reactions
are odd:

For example:

i.

Father, I say,
it's time you
and I had a talk
about cash.
(We seldom talk
about cash, my
father and I.)
And, after that,
it's time you
and I had a talk
about sex.
(Alas he's a
profligate spendthrift.)

Embarrassed indeed
at the topics proposed
for our chat, he neatly
avoids my net:

      "Is Herman around?"

ii.

Marguertite Hansel
comes at once to the point.
(I love her for this.)
Coming at once to the point
(in negligee and perfumed—
I love her for this…
      It's the coy
      smile that
      gets me)

      "You sure we're alone?"

iii

And then Arzeno-Kirkpatrick—
He's down the hall for a visit
and drunk

Surprised,
(Arzeno-Kirkpatrick's
often surprised)
he excuses
himself
and withdraws.

3

If everyone
would please
put down
his knife
and fork

                         she said

Herman would like to say grace.

4.

Out in her boat we were
and at night—
                rowing.

Not so dark, as I recall,
quarter moon and low white clouds?

You follow of course.

It was *her* boat.

She in the bow,
I at the oars,
In *her* boat.

> *On the other side*
> *she said*
> *once we reach the shore*
> *there I am yours.*

In *her* cabin, she meant.
In *her* bed.

That would be nice.
That would be nice, I said.

All in all
it was a pleasant night…

she in the bow,
I at the oars,
and Herman…

Herman catching crabs.

5

> *The time's going to come*
>   *she said*
> *The time's going to come*
>   *she intoned*
> *The time is most assuredly*
>   *nearly upon us*

When

Damn it all John

> *you bloody well have to*
> *bloody well chose:*
> *me or that Herman,*

Boojum

Arzeno Kirkpatrick

Should he, if the telephone rings,
pick it up? And if a knock should
come at the door? He ponders, Arzeno
Kirpatrick, the questions. Another
occurs: what if a light should
suddenly flash in the yard?
It is late; Arzeno Kirkpatrick
is tired. He sips his tea and
smokes his cigarettes. He
ponders, Arzeno Kirkpatrick,
the questions.

There is a light in the yard.
The telephone rings.
There is an angry knocking at the door.

The Crazy Side of the Room

Nowhere to
Be on
The crazy
Side of
The room
      I was looking
      And looking
      For Ilya Petrovich
Ah, for the wise and
Ferocious loon of
a slav
      Banging the giant
      Whore nor plucking
      The harp was
      Ilya Petrovich; no, nor
      Attending to who
      Should attend the
      Alchemical lectures.
I managed—which is
Some consolation—to
Find and engage in
Philosophical chat
The obese and distinguished
Japanese violinist
      Finally I said:
      Where in
      The name
      Of god is
      Petrovich?

Gone at last
To the wars?

Song for a David Isele Setting

a dazzle once
      was everything
and everywhere
      was fine:

      and dimmed
it all:
      day and the
dazzling
      dark:

      what shim-
mering a shim-
      mering of
sky:
      what shim-
mering a shim-
      mering of
sea:

      away and away

I peel tangerines
and walk away

A Dazzle

Three Love Songs for U.P.I.

i.m. Karl Kraus

1.

The army told congressmen yesterday it has enough of a single nerve gas in its chemical biological warfare arsenal to kill the world's population many times over. But Russia, one lawmaker reported, may harbor an even more lethal capability in this little discussed and highly secret field. The substance is labeled by the army "G.B." and the world's population is estimated at around 3-4 billion. Rep. Robert L.F. Sikes, D-Fla, said he thinks the U.S. is not doing enough in the field. Sikes said it is estimated the Russians have "seven to eight times" the capability of the United States. The U.S. has enough "G.B." to kill the world's estimated population about 30 times. Russia, on the other hand, has enough to kill the world's estimated population, say, 160 to 190 times.

2.

A hippie type amateur taxidermist was ordered held without bail on murder charges yesterday in the mutilation deaths of two of four women whose bodies were found in shallow graves in this Cape Cod community. The hearts were missing from the dismembered bodies. Even as police searched the scrub pine studded sandy wasteland for any more bodies, Antone Costa, 24, a currently unemployed sometimes carpenter with a literary fondness for existentialist authors, was arraigned in nearby Provincetown, a summer artists' mecca and hippie hangout. After his court appearance which attracted an overflow crowd including a number of hippies, Costa was committed to Bridgewater State Hospital for 35 days of observation. A plea of innocent to two murder counts was entered on his behalf. Costa, short and slight, with mustache, sideburns and semi-mod hairstyle wearing "granny" glasses, was taken to the courthouse after Dist. Atty. Edmund S. Dinis disclosed the grisly details in the case. About the hearts we'll say: I ate them for my dinner.

3.

Nomadic tribesmen claimed today under oath that the largest known most savory dish is stuffed roast camel, frequently served at Bedouin weddings. Hard-boiled eggs are stuffed into chickens stuffed in a sheep to finally be stuffed up the ass of a disemboweled camel. Rep. Robert L.F. Sikes, D-Fla, said he thinks the U.S. is not doing enough in this little discussed and highly secret field. Sikes said the Nomads have "seven to eight times" our number of Bedouin chefs. Bedouin chefs estimate the world's population at around 3.4 billion. Were there anywhere near that number of camels they might, according to Nomads, serve at their weddings the stuffed roast hearts of district attorneys.

Statement

Once upon a time Ezra Pound, when he was still a young man, not so young he was still an Imagist, but still young enough that he was a Vorticist, once upon a time ol' Ez had him a friend called Gaudier-Brzeska. Now this Gaudier, this Gaudier-Brzeska who was a friend of Ezra Pound's (Pound the vorticist—always honoring craft) this Gaudier was a craftsman of genius—a sculptor. He worked on stone with his hands, and his hands were trained—trained hands. I mean the man knew what he did, didn't hack it with cudgels and hammers, didn't just kick it or punch it, he sculpted the stone with his exquisite perfectly trained controlled and controlling hands. (If, for example, the man had liked violin, he would have taken the time to find out where one puts down one's fingers. If, for example, the man had liked the cooking of pastries, he would have learned from a pastry cook how to cook pastries. If, for example, the man had liked carpentry, he would have learned that screws hold under certain kinds of stresses where nails don't—etc. etc.) But his medium was stone. And he was a craftsman of genius—of genius. He had learned his craft, do you follow me. And that turned out (it does turn out, if you're serious, but most people aren't) to spell the difference between freedom and slavery, or, to be more precise in the parable, between freedom and imprisonment. "The instincts are not free springs of connation towards a goal. They are, so far as they can be abstractly separated, unconscious necessities, as Kant realized. They are unfree. But in their realization as behaviour, when these innate things-in-themselves become things-for-themselves and interact with their environment (which also changes and is not the dead world of physics) they also change. Above all, they are changed in human culture. As a result of this change, these necessities become conscious, become emotion and thought; they exist for themselves and are altered thereby. The change is the emotion or thought, and now they are no longer the instincts, for they are conscious and consciousness is not an ethereal but a material determining relationship. The necessity that is conscious is not the necessity that is unconscious. The conscious goal is different from the blind instinctive goal. It is freer." So then Gaudier. Gaudier choosing craft and consciousness, choosing freedom. So then Gaudier—Gaudier refusing to be enslaved by refusing to know, Gaudier refusing imprisonment. But they tried, the governments and their jailers, they tried, the governments and jailers unconscious and therefore unfree, to jail, in the war, this conscious spirit, this Gaudier. But Gaudier loved freedom, and because he loved freedom learned craft. Because he loved freedom learned craft so perfectly that he became a craftsman of genius. And his medium was stone. Stone were the jails of the governments and the jailers. Stone was his medium—a genius with exquisite perfectly trained controlled and controlling hands. Free hands. Free because they knew craft. Jails, Penitentiaries, Sanatoriums, all made out of stone. Stone walls, many feet thick. Stone jails. Jail-thick stone walls where they put him, craftsman and free, they—the governments making their wars.

Minutes after they threw him there in his cell, minutes after they locked him in that cage of stone, Gaudier, Pound's friend the Vorticist, took, with his bare hands, and eight-foot-thick wall apart and went home.

Missed Call

The phone was off the hook.
Qualified professionals
Ignored the trunk. It lay
On its chest. The wrists
Were bound with tape.
These men had things to do
And lightly stepped.

The phone was off the hook.
The elevator door was jammed.
Legs and hips lay bleeding
In a chair.
On a landing of
The spiral stair
A matron washed
The head.
She washed it in a pan.

And the manager said:
He tried to get out.
He tried to ring you up.
The phone was off the hook.
The elevator door was jammed.

Graffiti Gratis Bon Obscène Maudit d'Autrefois

1

Johnson, Nixon
and Agnew meet
in my kitchen at six.
Each declares he
wants to kick my ass.
I'm all at sea until
Daley arrives with
bananas. "I have the
bananas," he says.
Johnson, Nixon and
Agnew peel their
bananas. Daley
declares he wants to
kick my ass.

2.

The scene suddenly
shifts to the House
of Lords. Which isn't
a house at all but a
kitchen. I'm given
a ceremonial blanket
to sit on…
      The shout goes up:
            HE'S SLIDING INTO THE LORDS!
            HE'S SLIDING INTO THE LORDS!

3.

I'm due to meet
Chairman Mao in
Hanoi. (Hanoi
is really a kitchen.)

"I have," I declare,
"the ceremonial blanket."
    The shout does up:
          AND CHAIRMAN MAO HAS GOT
              THE BANANAS.

(Actual prophetic dream of *poète maudit* François Villon [1431-1968], here freely translated from the French by Robert Lowell.)

Short Parts of a Long Poem

...

Korok.

And of Korok, Kazi or Brelum
Teka or Tecta.

Libushka. Libushka
of Korok, a sybil.

Weleska said: Our lady
Libushka is dead.

But let us continue to rule.

.

The tithes were refused.
The clergymen were assaulted.
Henry IV deferred to
the Bishop of Bremen.

Excommunicate (about '97)
and damned, the men
of that region deferred
to the women.

.

Hordes of devils are making for France!
(The French, you know, are
a restless and turbulent people.)
Run the country in absence
of husband and son?
Libushka of Korok, a sybil.

.

A toad the size of a goose or a duck.
The rhetoric of crusades.

...

The knocked-up look is back!
(old accurate Van Eyck):
the turned-up pointd shoes,
the twin-peaked cap.
Gentlemen, there's no one
here but Gentlemen.

And ladies.

And the court.

Virgins of St. Denis
bare their privies for
the prince. And I am priest
and altar, consecrated host.
Bread and whisky on
my loins, a wooden
phallus, nails:
I stiffen and endure.

Empty out the coffins, then.

Disinter the bones.

...

It has come to our ears that numbers of
both sexes do not avoid to have
intercourse
                  and he said it has come to our ears

to have intercourse (fucking) with
incubi succubi demons on
Saturday nights / He was found in a posture!

Viz. On a stool by the hearth of the
chimney His feet on the floor his
body straight upward his shoulders
touching the lintel. And they by
their sorceries charm incantations
(and plagiaries) cause to expire
(extinguish) to parish (they suffocate!)
children of women increase of
animals corn of the ground grapes
of the vineyard fruit of the trees
as well as the men and the women
the flocks and the herds and all
other various kinds and kinds.

Viz. On a stool by the hearth.

Tied (his neck) with his
neck-cloth (whereof the
knot was behind) to a small
stick thrust in a hole in
the lintel. Having the strength
to bear the weight of
his body? His struggle?
Making procuring to blast
torment within and without.
That he could never have
been the actor himself. An agent
had done it: extraordinary, bizarre.

The door of the room was secured.

The human circle turns:

Widdershins.

...
                    wes cled in
a black gown
with a blak hat
vpon his

his faice was

his noise lyk

lyk the bek of ane egle gret bournyng

of an egle gret bournyng his eyn / His handis
and leggis wer herry Hes handis with clawes
His feit lyk / Wes cled in
vpon his

       Agnes Sampson

Agnes Sampson recording, official, brief: he had on
a gown and a hat that were both black. *Thank you.*
Thank you very much.

    ...

      somtym he vold be
      lyk a stirk
      lyk a bukk
      lyk a rae
      lyk a deir
      lyk a dowg
      He vould hold wp his taill: Lo!
      we kiss his arce.

Thank you
Thank you very much

    ...

and stript her there

a thing like
udder of a ewe
that giveth suck
two teats behind
her armhole there
her privie parts
and there as well
a teat a finger-length
and hairy
and

           deliver me

they searched her body found upon her cunt a lump
about the bigness of a nut and wett and then they wrung
it with their fingers there and moisture came like lee

...

a lantern there

or candle-light
I couldn't tell
a light a
phosphorescence there
a presence
and

I danced

a sound of pleasant instruments
a violin and pipes
a tambourine
and singing there

around the great gray stone
and through the painted
gate obscured by fog
a semi-circle then
a circle formed
and Him astride
the first of us
inside

One by one inside that ring
He took

and marked them there

...

in the kirk yard / with her daughters adoring

His member

                        exceeding great and long / no manis
memberis so great and long / is abler for us then
than ony man could bee / is heavie lyk a stone and
verie cold as yce

                      and stript her there

...

Gentlemen that gentleman
disappears in the east
cultivates beautiful manners
beautiful women…
Engraves a heavy silver ring
With cabalistic signs

        Pious and elegant ladies

            there
At the Alloway kirk

(Father, confess me
for I am pretty and blonde.)

(*Bagabi! Lamac! Samahac!*
She didn't *say* she was twelve
didn't say she wanted to
cultivate beautiful manners)

        reappears in Suffolkshire…

    …told of
lonely roads: the others
walking in silence: a
bleating voice calling
from forest and plain.
(From the tips of her toes
to the crown of her head she
bathed herself with oil.

Then he took her quickly in the nave

…

                        love
is license / All
the women his
everybody manic or possessed
In cities of renunciation
flagellants make law:
ecstasy makes criminals of girls.
Charges! Guilty!
Fili Redemptor . . .)

                harden (oh, cannot) his hardest heart
Charges easy:
horny gods in trees:
every carnal field
a carnal synagogue
in May
        Kobal! Nibbas!
Chancellor Adramaleck!
Emissaries, dignitaries: post.

Gentlemen, when exorcism fails,
drive along the highway to the coast…

I drove along the highway to the coast: Under sixty all the while and looking sharp. I had memorized directions; I had memorized my lines. I knew exactly where to go and what I'd say. No pants. No bra. I felt myself to be sure. I recited like a bull and like a dog. There was fog in patches and I dimmed the lights. Suddenly a figure there ahead. I parked by the side of the road and stared: rigid, scared

always this initial inclination to refuse

always inclination, always to refuse

who'd offer even now (in 1968) the choiring chymic cure

…

pale and black, unparfyt whyte and red,
pekoks feathers (color gay) and rainbow
which shall overgoe the spottyd panther
with the lyon.
                     croys byll blue as lede:

Mix and treat in philosopher's egg

    .

Bird of Hermes
Goose of Hermogenes
two-edged sword in the hand of the Cherub
chirping in the tree of life . . .

Mix and treat in philosophr's egg

(one the ram)

one the ram / one the ram / one the ram / one the ram / one the ram
one the ram / one the ram

       …and Oedipus said
       to the Sphinx:

       for a square of
       the elements in
       essence is
       triangular

       the hemisphere's
       two lines are
       straight and
       curved

the hieroglyphic figure
a dragon bites his tail
an emerald table and
the elemental sprite
the greater magistry
the humid path
the lesser magistry
the mystical drama of good
the composition of astra
the polarity of their molecules
the elements to which it belongs
the banner of Harpocrates
scion you congeal from 8 & 10
enigma and acrostic
the colors of the king
ubiquity of the end
primitive and proximate
the igneous principle there
the matrix of its acts
the value is 192
little cohesion draws
convex mirrors concave screens
a tingling metalline spirit
448, 344
acapulco gold lysergicade
an organ with seven pipes and an altar
rings on their fingers
swords with silver hilts
fine gay gloves on their hands
256, 224
to lie upon the primal waters
darkness of the world
a year in hiding or an influential friend
to undertake no study
the salt remains in the ash
the death of a man
the death, indeed, of a metal
take corporeal form
hidden by light
the severed heads of crows
a saffron-colored candle in the sky

such harmony / and yet this muddy vesture of decay

...

(tripod over flame) Doth not attempt to transmute
into gold but summon Thoth o ibis-headed god o Mercury
(Tripod over flame) Doth not attempt to transmute into
gold but summon Thoth o ibis-
                                  headed god o Mercury of
churning elements hermaphrodite (tripod over flame) Doth
not attempt to transmute into gold but summon Thoth o
ibis-headed god o Mercury of churning elements
hermaphrodite and over hell in flask a
wingèd dragon call (tripod over
flame) Doth not attempt to
transmute into gold
but summon Thoth o
ibis-headed
god
          o Mercury of churning elements hermaphrodite and
over hell in flask a wingèd dragon call doth not
attempt to transmute into gold (tripod over flame)
doth not attempt to transmute into gold is no vain
cauldron-cook or chemist but for Thoth will sweat
        whole days and nights before that
                furnace until face explode in boils
                          and running sores (tripod over flame)
doth not attempt to transmute into gold
        is no vain cauldron-cook or chemist but for Thoth
                will sweat whole days and nights
before that furnace until face
explode in boils and running
soars his fingers burn in
coals and clay and filth to
summon Thoth o ibis-headed god
o Mercury of churning
elements hermaphrodite
and over hell
in flask
a winged dragon call

(which shall be a sign unto you)

Whether the canons were ever intended to be sung whilst alchemical experiments were being carried out cannot be determined with any degree of certainty. The actual bearing of the words on procedures is by no means clear, although both incantation and ritual action would seem to call for consummate skill. It is difficult to believe that singers possessing the necessary musical and scientific knowledge could be found amongst the laboratory assistants of the time; it certainly would not be possible to find such assistants today

        (matter, he said,
        expresses mysterious sound

        music coeval with speech

        number
        weight
        and measure

        chymic harps

Notes

Putting together this last volume of my Shearsman *Collected Poems* (which is chronologically the first) leaves me in many ways—and therefore almost certainly my reader—with more questions than answers. This is no bad thing. Often enough questions about a poet's body of work—especially if he has been lucky enough to have lived at least to his Biblical allotment of threescore years and ten and to have published consistently during much of that time—are more interesting than the answers sometimes put forward over-confidently by a self-collecting author. Who at seventy knows what to make of a poem that he wrote at twenty? And yet make something of it the poet must if he is doing this business of gathering his poems together himself. I in fact tried early on in the process of foraging and rootling around in old books and manuscripts to pass on the whole chore to Robert Archambeau, my one-time student, good friend, astute critic, and (ultimately) my executor. Although Archambeau will one day get the final say in all this, he very tactfully declined to perform the editorial task while I am still in a position to cast a veto on his decisions.

So what is a poet to do about his earliest work, especially if he began to publish when very young? My first journal publications began while I was still an undergraduate. Certain lines, and in one case an entire poem, I have saved from before I was twenty. These early poems—most but by no means all from *Bucyrus* (1970) and two chapbooks (*Other Poems* and *Herman's Poems*)—appear at the beginning and end of the book. This may appear to be a rather odd strategy, but there are two ways to think about "earliness," and this ordering of things suggests what they may be. I have included a few poems built from the passages I mentioned above. I have stitched a few things together, and I have written some new lines in a few of the first poems that appear. In the last section, 'I gather the bones of *Bucyrus*,' I have excerpted certain passages from the first two sections of the original 'Poem in Three Parts' which appeared at the end of that book. In some ways I like the last section of that early long poem best, but stylistically it is nothing more than a pastiche of Charles Olson. As for the title piece (which in fact is written in prose), I now agree with what Mark Scroggins once wrote in a review in which he said that 'Bucyrus' is weird. "Not good weird," he went on, "just weird."

The middle sections of the book (II, III, IV) are semi-chronological, with poems overlapping that first appeared in *Turns* (1970), *Crossing* (1979), *Northern Summer* (1984), and in various magazines during these and the next several years. In shuffling together stylistically compatible or complementary poems from a period getting on to three decades, I am nonetheless representing a coherent period of composition, the period during which I wrote mostly during the summers in England. The East Anglian region, in particular, became important to me over the years, and many of the poems in these sections deal with historical, geographical, topological, and cultural matters which I would probably never have cared or written about had I not lived for a long time both in Cambridge and in my wife's family home near the Aldeburgh coast in Suffolk. The lines from Vladeta Vučković's *The Dimensions* and a group of lyrics by Branko Milković constitute a "free translation and recombination" modeled on the pieces from Octavio Paz that were composed much earlier but are nonetheless best printed now beside these others that use the same method. Section V is a series of "found" monologues followed by texts for a song cycle. The music actually printed in Parts I and VI is by David Clark Isele—settings of 'Between' and 'A Dazzle Once' which appear as two of Isele's *Four Songs for Voices* (2000). My thanks to the composer and E.C. Schirmer Music Company for permission to reprint the scores. As I have said, the last section of the book returns to beginnings. But *Bucyrus* is not quite Osirus, and bones are not quite limbs. Still, it is interesting to rattle them a bit in the medicine-bag of this coda.

§

One takes what one needs, but with thanks and praise. I have plundered various sources as indicated below (1) to get my general bearings in the course of a composition or (2) for passages and fragments which provide documentary material in which poetic energy can be isolated so as to expand the voicing of particular parts of this book—sometimes quoting, sometimes translating or transmuting them (vide 'Turns'). A poet's often random, pretty unscholarly (though sometimes purposeful) reading over certain periods of time when engaged in assembling certain kinds of structures.

Part I. Nello Ponente, *Klee: Biographical and Critical Study*; Erwin Mitsche, *Egon Schiele: Drawings and Water-Colours*; David Isele, 'Between,' *Songs for Four Voices*; Anon, 'Edward,' Osip Mandelstam, the Stalin epigram; Nadezhda Mandelstam, *Hope Against Hope*; John Garvick, table talk; tags from Yeats, Joyce, de Sade, Octavio Paz, Marianne Moore, John Cocteau.

Part II: Gunnar Ekelöf, 'Xoanan,' cf. p.232; Göran Sonnevi, 'Tomrum som faller...' from *Ingrepp-modeller*; Lars Norén, 'Augusti' from *Viltspeglar*; F.S. Howes, *The English Musical Renaissance*; R.B. Dobson, ed., *The Peasants' Revolt of 1381*; Rodney Hilton, *Bond Men Made Free*; Norman Cohn, *The Pursuit of the Millennium*; R.A. Edwards, *The Fighting Bishop*; Bryan Houghton, *Saint Edmund, King and Martyr*; Julian Tennyson, *Suffolk Scene*; Sir Geoffrey Keynes, ed., *Sir Thomas Browne: Selected Writings*; W.G. Arnot, *Orwell Estuary*; George Ewart Evans, *Ask the Fellows Who Cut the Hay*; Julia Pipe, *Port on the Alde*; Rudyard Kipling, 'A Smuggler's Song'; Richard Cobbold, *The History of Margaret Catchpole*; Justin Kaplan, *Mr. Clemens and Mark Twain*; Mark Twain, 'The Celebrated Jumping Frog of Calavaras County'; Joana Richardson, *Verlaine*; Paul Verlaine, 'Sagesse'; Tacitus, *The Annals of Imperial Rome*, chapters 10 and 11; Stephen Gosson, *School of Abuse*; R.R. Clarke, *East Anglia*, chapters 6 and 7; I.A. Richmond, *Roman Britain*, chapters 1, 2, and 5; Donald R. Dudley and Graham Webster, *The Rebellion of Boudicca*; Patrick Crampton, *Stonehenge of the Kings*, chapter 1; Ronald Blythe, ed., *An Aldeburgh Anthology*.

Part III: C.J. Stranks, *St. Etheldreda: Queen and Abbess*; *The Book of Margery Kempe*; Julian of Norwich, *Revelations of Divine Love*; P. Franklin Chambers, *Juliana of Norwich: An Introductory and Interpretive Anthology*; Joan Poulson, *Old Anglian Recipes*; César Vallejo, 'Agape'; Johann Huizinga, *Homo Ludens*; *The Manual of Horsemanship of the Brtitish Horse Society and Pony Club*; Lars Norén, 'Autumn'; tags from Robert Lowell, John Berryman, W.B. Yeats, Woody Allen, Robert Hass, Wordsworth, King Lear, Mark Twain, Paul Verlaine, Rudyard Kipling, Edmund Burke; Thomas Hardy, *Jude the Obscure*; H.T. Low Porter, translator's note, Thomas Mann's *Doctor Faustus*; A.F.E. Burroughs, *West Midland Dialects of the 14th Century*; J. Matthias, 'Th' Entencioun and Spech of Philosophers'; tags from King Alfred, Chaucer, Langland, John of Mandeville, Wycliffe, the *Pearl* poet, Joseph of Arimathaea; George Steiner, *Language and Silence*; *The Great Tournament Roll of Westminster, A Collotype Reproduction of the Manuscript*: Sydney Anglo's Historical Introduction, Appendices I and II—*Tiptoft's Ordinances and the Revels Account of Richard Gibson*, and the *Analytical Description*; Gordon Donaldson, *Scottish Kings*; Lt. Colonel Howard Green, *Battlefields of Britain and Ireland*; Peter Alexander, Introduction to Shakespeare's (?) *Henry VIII* in *The Collins Tudor Shakespeare*.

Part IV: Edmund Wilson, *To the Finland Station*; Kurt Seligmann, *A History of Magic*; Paul Hindemith, Libretto: *Mathis der Maler*; Otto Benesch, *The Art of the Renaissance in Northern Europe*, chapter II; Ian Kemp, *Hindemith*; F.W. Sternfeld, ed., *Music in the Modern Age*, chapter 2. 'Germany,' Elaine Padmore; Norman Cohn, *The Pursuit of the Millennium*; John Matthias and Vladeta Vučković, trans., *The Battle of Kosovo*; Vladeta Vučković, *The Dimensions*; Branko Miljković, 'Pohvala Vatri' and other poems; Jacques Dupin, 'L'Egyptienne' and 'L'Urne'; Knut Hamsun, *Hunger*; Octavio Paz, 'Salamandra' and 'Ladera Este'; François Villon, 'L'Epitaphe Villon'; Margaret Thatcher on The Falklands, quoted in *Le Monde*; Neil Lands, *The French Pyrenees*; E. Cortade, *Collioure: Guide Historique et Touristique*; Yves Bonnefoy, 'Jean et Jeanne'; Antonio Machado, 'El sol es un globo de fuego'; Guiraud Riquier, 'Be'm degra de chantar tener'; Stéphane Mallarmé, 'Prose—pour des Esseintes.'

Part V: Joseph Swetnam, 'Epistle to the Reader' and 'Preface to Professors' in *The Noble Science of Defence*; George Silver, *The Paradoxes of Defence* and *Brief Instructions Upon My Paradoxes of Defence*; J.D. Aylward, *The English Masters of Arms*; A.L. Soens, 'Lawyers, Collusions and Cudgels: Middleton's Anything For a Quiet Life', I.i. 220-221, *English Language Notes*, Vol. VI, No. 4; Henry John Temple Palmerston, 'Cambridge Spinning House: Rules and Regulations, 1854'; Sir John Rothenstein, *Modern British Painters*, Vols. 1, 2, and 3; Jeremy Bentham, The Will; Heinrich Heine, 'Der Doppelgänger'; Aeschylus, *Agamemnon*; Euripides, *Iphigenia in Aulis*; George Seferis, 'Euripides the Athenian'; Gunnar Ekelöf, 'Xoanon.' Ekelöf wrote the following to Leif Sjöberg about the icon which was in his possession: "Basically she is an old Xoanon made of olive wood, an olive plank, dead, on which the icon is painted. She is standing here on my chest of drawers by the way, and she always has flowers near her. She is constructed in such a way as to make it possible to undress her—the child (on a stool, standing, in a Byzantine emperor's garments), the veil, the cloak, the seven arrows of pain in her left breast, yes, the breasts and the stomach and the arms and everything until you get to the holy tree, which you could not fell in Attica with impunity." *Xoanon*, ancient wooden image in Greek temples, icon; *Panayía*: Greek, "Our Lady"; *Basmá*, a repousée metal (usually silver) covering over some icons, allowing only the face and hands to be seen; *Maphorion*, a veil-like headdress covering head and shoulders of all female saints and the Virgin Mary; *Hodigítria*, "The Guide," Mother of

God icon; *Philoúsa*, "Loving Virgin," Mother of God icon.

Part VI: Margaret A. Murray, *The World of the Witches*; Jules Michelet, *Satanism and Witchcraft*; John Reid, *Narrative of the Sufferings of a Young Girle*; Jean Lhermitte, *True and False Possession*; Julio Caro Baroja, *The World of the Witches*; Kurt Seligmann, *The History of Magic*; John Read, *Prelude to Chemistry*; Carl Jung, "The Idea of Redemption in Alchemy," *The Integration of the Personality*; Frederic Spiegelberg, *Alchemy as a Way of Salvation*; F.H. Sawyer, 'The Music in "Atalanta Fugiens"'; Geoffrey Chaucer, 'The Canon's Yeoman's Tale'; John Matthias, 'Th'Entencoun and Speche of Philosophers' (unpublished); Jacobus Sprenger and Heinrich Kramer, *Malleus Maleficarum*; Max Marwick, ed., *Witchcraft and Sorcery*; A.E. Waite, ed., *The Hermetic Museum* and *The Hermetic and Alchemical Writings of Paracelsus*; tags and fragments from Paracelsus, Basil Valentine, Roger Bacon, Petrus Bonus, Albertus Magnus, Cornelius Agrippa, Norton, Asmole, Ripley, Chaucer, et al. Passages deriving from alchemical texts and the witchcraft trials are mostly a modified cento of recombined materials.

Readers of my work have sometimes asked me to write "more extensive notes" for my poems. I understand the frustration, especially given the mid-Atlantic nature of a lot that I have written. American readers may not recognize one set of references, British readers may not recognize another. Although I have reprinted only the original bibliographical notes in this and the other two volumes of my Shearsman collected poems, I will add here what might be an example of a "more extensive note" to one of the poems included here in order to suggest, if nothing else, what questions of length, expense, and tact would be involved. Only David Jones has really mastered the art of opening up "unshared backgrounds"—or even, as one must now say, "unshared foregrounds"—in notes. The following was put together for a BBC Radio 3 broadcast of '26 June 1381/1977.'

Henry Despenser (or le Despenser, or Lespenser—the name is given a French pronunciation in the seventeenth line) was Bishop of Norwich during the period of the Peasants' Revolt and put down an East Anglian version of that insurrection in the fields of North Walsham on 26 June 1381. The leader of the Norfolk revolt, Geoffrey Lidster (or Litster, or Litester), a dyer by trade, was defeated, tried, and confessed by Despenser, who then followed him as he was dragged behind a wagon to the place of execution, trying to keep the condemned man's head from bouncing on the road. For putting down the revolt the Norfolk nobles gave Despenser the famous painted retable or reredos, now in Norwich Cathedral, which was restored by Pauline Plummer in 1958. The poem has to do with the revolt, the execution of Lidster, the painting of the reredos, the restoration of the reredos, and with various reactions to these events. A fragment from one of the allegorical letters of protest which circulated during the Peasants' Revolt is quoted in the poem, as is the well-known rhyme of the period about Adam and Eve. Though in point of historical fact Despenser's brass has disappeared, we know that the epitaph included the words *miles amatus* and *boni pastoris mens*—"beloved soldier" and "the soul of this good shepherd." I should perhaps add that malachite and azurite were used in the restoration of the anonymous Norwich master's painting of the last events in the life of Christ, and that the restorer had to replace entirely the head and arms of Christ on the cross in the wooden center panel.

www.ingramcontent.com/pod-product-compliance
Lightning Source LLC
Chambersburg PA
CBHW032125160426
43197CB00008B/519